SHAKESPEARE'S IMAGES OF PREGNANCY

SHAKESPEARE'S IMAGES OF PREGNANCY

Elizabeth Sacks

St. Martin's Press

New York

ISBN 0-312-71595-1

Library of Congress Cataloging in Publication Data

Sacks, Elizabeth Merilynne.
  Shakespeare's images of pregnancy.

  Bibliography: p.
  Includes index.
  1. Shakespeare, William, 1564-1616—Style.
2. Pregnancy in literature.   I.   Title.
PR3069.P74S2   822.3'3   80-15559
ISBN 0-312-71595-1

. . . any understanding knoweth the skil of the Artificer standeth in that *Idea* or fore-conceite of the work, and not in the work it selfe. And that the Poet hath that *Idea* is manifest, by delivering them forth in such excellencie as he hath imagined them. Which delivering forth also is not wholly imaginative, as we are wont to say by them that build Castles in the ayre: but so farre substantially it worketh, not only to make a *Cyrus*, which had been but a particuler excellencie, as Nature might have done, but to bestow a *Cyrus* upon the *worlde*, to make many *Cyrus's*, if they wil learne aright why and how that Maker made him.

Sir Philip Sidney,
An Apologie for Poetrie (1595)

And what of all this; Marry, read the booke and you shall know; but read nothing except you read all. And why so? Because the beginning shows not the middle, and the middle shows not the latter end.

Thomas Deloney,
The Gentle Craft (1648 edn)

For my parents, Dr and Mrs David Sacks,
and for my husband, Fred Chase

Contents

Preface

This study evolved from a longstanding interest in the 'life-force' suffusing Shakespeare's work. What is it, I wondered, which renews his appeal for every generation? Originally I focused on performance, exploring contrasted aspects of doing and non-doing in the fools and philosophers. There was Touchstone, about to marry his Audrey; there was Hamlet, throwing off Ophelia and heading toward the grave. My emphasis shifted to the relationship between *sexual* performance and action. A detailed study of *Measure for Measure*, which forms the core of this book, revealed that the creative principle in Shakespeare is rooted in pregnancy, whether literal, figurative, or both simultaneously. I reread all the plays, and there it was: pregnancy underlining key themes, permeating the imagery, vivifying the characters. Colleagues' initial scepticism ('I didn't know Shakespeare had any children') turned to interest ('I never thought of it *that* way'), and the embryonic project took rapid shape.

An analysis of creativity such as this cannot hope to cover everything, and, much as I have tried to clarify in succeeding pages the range and impact of pregnancy in Shakespeare, there will be those who feel that something is missing. To them I answer that, as far as our understanding of Shakespeare goes, much indeed is missing. When we study Shakespeare, we study our origins, and if this work lifts the curtain on some part of the great mystery, it has fulfilled its aim.

Thanks to those professors who assisted me in research: Paul Jorgensen, Edward Condren, Michael Allen, Ynez O'Neill; and to those who offered valuable suggestions in revision: Robert Kinsman, Juliet Dusinberre and Alan Roper. I gratefully acknowledge the kind assistance of T. M. Farmiloe at Macmillan Press Ltd. To my colleagues Ellen Caldwell, Lisa Weston and Trevor Thomas, *mille remerciements*. To my friends Colin Gardner and Ken Klimak, who encouraged this project from its early days, and Mark

Minato, who helped with the final proofing, I cry gramercy. I follow a long tradition in paying tribute to the fortitude of my spouse, Fred, who has borne all without a murmur, even if with the occasional scream. The Sacks/Krausz family is a constant source of inspiration and support; I acknowledge the encouragement of Dr Oliver Sacks and the memory of Dr Elsie Landau (Sacks).

In quoting from Shakespeare, I use *The Complete Plays and Poems of William Shakespeare*, ed. William Allen Neilson and Charles Jarvis Hill (Cambridge, Mass.: Houghton Mifflin, 1942). Holofernes's *pia mater* passage, quoted in the discussion of *Love's Labour's Lost* (ch. 2), is drawn from the New Arden edition of the play, ed. Richard David (London: Methuen, 1968). All *Measure for Measure* citations also refer to the New Arden edition, ed. J. W. Lever (London: Methuen, 1967). For *The Two Noble Kinsmen*, I use G. L. Proudfoot's edition (Lincoln, Nebr.: University of Nebraska Press, 1970). I am grateful to Fredric Cook, of the Los Angeles Academy of Dramatic Art, for allowing quotation of his material in Chapter 2.

For all primary sources, I mostly retain original spelling and punctuation. Occasional emendation includes the standardisation of i/j and u/v in accordance with modern usage, and the reversal of any other than emphatic italics.

Elizabeth Sacks

Los Angeles
April 1980

1 Preconceptions

The most creative mental act that we can perform is to have an original idea; our most creative physical act is to have a child. Our physical universe enables us to express with comparative ease the actual generative process, but we lack the spiritual vocabulary to describe the ideational process. Man uses aspects of his physical experience as metaphors to compass the indescribably spiritual. In the human frame of reference, an idea itself is a quality to be *digested*. Lacking the language to think in utter abstract, we raid our lexicon of concrete terms in order to express the inexpressible. This appropriation is most evident in the identical terminology which we use to describe the production of children and brainchildren. Or, to put it another way, a significant area of semantic and cultural reference exists in the punning tension of the expressions used to define the highest physical and mental function: the creation of an original.

'Conception' may refer to the engendering of a child or of an idea, and, when we admit the existence of this pun, two loci of human 'pregnancy' present themselves. Man can generate literally below the waist or figuratively in his head. The metaphor of generation is so instinctive to us that the etymology of 'concept' goes largely unremarked. Our commonest idioms reveal the extraordinary pervasiveness of this metaphor. We refer to an *abortive* idea, the *birth* of a project (formerly, perhaps, in *embryo*). A *brainchild* is the natural *issue* of a *fertile* mind, sometimes *delivered*, with great *labour*, after a *pregnant* pause. An unrealised idea may be said to be in *gestation*. As we shape our experiences anew, our minds *conceive*. Is the *conception* viable? Literally: 'Can the baby survive outside the womb?'

The generation metaphor, supreme expression of creativity, is the most accessible of verbal images, possessing a universal appeal which explains its lasting popularity in creation myths. The intimate connection between literal and figurative pregnancy – in fact, a view of them as identical – informs Timothy Bright's account of the Creation, together with the origin of the human soul:

1

If you demaunde whereof this Spirit is made? I take it to be an effectuall, and pregnant substance, bred in all thinges, at what time the spirit of the Lord did, as it were, hatch, and breede out all living thinges, out of that Chaos mentioned in Genesis; which Chaos, as it was matter of corporall, and palpable substance to all thinges; so did it also minister this lively Spirit unto them, diverse and severall, according to the diversitie of those seedes, which God indued it withall: to some more pure: to other some more grosse . . . from this power of God, sprang the Spirite of man.[1]

Several interesting points emerge from this account. First, the generating Spirit of the Lord moves upon the face of the waters in Genesis, and there the Hebrew word for this force, *ruach*, means both 'spirit' and 'wind'. Wind, of course, is related to breath. The creation of mankind is an act of in-*spir*-ation: the vital spirit, breath of life, is blown into him. Hence the stock Renaissance simile comparing human life to a bubble or breath.[2] The primal Inspiration, hatching life out of the deep, creates a human spirit which is itself fundamentally creative: 'effectuall, and pregnant'. Man has a fertile mind, planted in him by the first fertile mind. This account of human origin *via* divine cerebral conception was hardly without precedent: Athene sprang from Zeus's head,[3] and at least one myth of creation features prime generator and generatrix thinking hard and producing humanity.[4]

Sex, the necessary prelude to conception, also possesses an important figurative meaning, referrable to mental activity. We inherit a fearsomely earthy legacy from Adam and Eve, whose first act of knowledge, outside of knowing the naked truth, was to 'know' each other sexually;[5] the Hebrew term, *yada*, conveys both senses. In his great manifesto, *The Advancement of Learning* (1605), Francis Bacon equates sex with cognition, using the metaphor to express an ideal relationship between man and knowledge: 'Knowledge may not be as a Curtezan for pleasure, & vanitie only, or as a bond-woman to acquire and gaine to her Masters use, but as a Spouse, for generation, fruit, and comfort.'[6] Thus a creative or inspired human soul, emulating the first omniscient Inspiration, is one in which knowledge acts as a fertilising power.

To the Renaissance, the process of human thought was a small-scale repetition of Genesis. Man could also be inspired and conceive. Specifically in the case of poets, that which needed to be inspired was the imagination – the image- or shape-producing faculty.[7] This concern manifests itself in abundant tributes to man's fertile imagination. Stephen Hawes describes the creation of something from nothing in *The Pastime of Pleasure* (1517):

> by ymagynacyon
> To drawe a mater / full facundyous
> Ful mervaylous / is the operacyon
> To make of nought / reason sentencyous.[8]

Indeed – the work of a truly fertile mind. The word 'facundyous' dominates Hawes's account of Rhetoric. Imagination is fecund, providing the base matter for rhetorical 'disposition' and apt utterance. The fertile power of imagination lies in its ability to bring forth eloquence in mankind. Sidney's *Defence of Poesie* (1595) claims imagination as the *sine qua non* of poets, who have the potential not only to recreate Nature, but also to improve upon it through the exercise of their art:

> the Poet . . . doth grow in effect into an other nature: in making things either better than nature bringeth foorth, or quite anew, formes such as never were in nature . . . he goeth hand in hand with nature, not enclosed within the narrow warrant of her gifts, but freely raunging within the Zodiack of his owne wit. . . her world is brasen, the Poets only deliver a golden. . . .

> Neither let it be deemed too sawcy a comparison, to ballance the highest point of mans wit, with the efficacie of nature: but rather give right honor to the heavenly maker of that maker, who having made man to his owne likenes, set him beyond and over all the workes of that second nature, which in nothing he sheweth so much as in Poetry; when with the force of a divine breath, he bringeth things foorth surpassing her doings.[9]

The true poet, then, is endowed with inspiration, that 'divine breath' which, like the Spirit of the Lord, creates new realities. Roger Ascham evinces a typically scholarly distrust of 'quick wittes', deploring their speed, heat, keenness, and other mercurial qualities. However, even Ascham, for whom quick wits were soon ripe, soon rotten, conceded that 'the quickest wittes commonlie may prove the best Poetes'.[10] 'Quick' literally means 'alive'.

Renaissance scientists held that imagination, along with understanding and memory, resided in the brain. Independent of the metaphor behind 'inspiration', which characterised man's soul as quick, vital and fertile, Renaissance medical teminology likened the brain to a womb. Folklore establishes as a feminine symbol 'anything that is cavernous, circular, concave, curving, hollow, oval, round'.[11] Mediaeval physicians had followed classical Arabic writers in generally calling the cavities of the brain 'ventricles',[12] a diminutive term which could mean either 'little belly' or 'little womb'. The Old English equivalent, *wamb*, also possessed both meanings. The two protective membranes sheltering the brain from the cranium were called *pia mater* and *dura mater* ('tender mother' and 'hard mother'), metaphorical names which lead us to a 'womb' reading for the word 'ventricle'. By extension, the brain becomes a locus of conception.

Certain metaphors inexplicably sink and surface during different literary periods. The English Renaissance was a particularly auspicious time for the metaphor of generation. It saw the 'dynastic crisis'[13] which plagued Henry VIII, and during Elizabeth's barren reign the same problem was no less keenly felt. Matters of birth and succession perplexed politicians for almost the entire sixteenth century and obtruded themselves upon the national subconscious. The English language itself was undergoing rebirth.[14] Rediscovery of the generation metaphor seemed appropriate, and proclaimed the new-found eloquence of the mother tongue in a time of relative prosperity, geographic exploration, and great literary productivity. In *Musophilus* (1599), Samuel Daniel hails poetry as the mother of eloquence:

> Poesie (mother of this force)
> That breeds, brings forth, and nourishes by this might,
> Teaching it in a loose, yet measured course
> With comely motions how to go upright:
> And fostring it with bountifull discourse
> Adorns it thus in fashions of delight.[15]

A syndrome which we may call 'male womb-envy' easily accounts for the popularity of this metaphor in the Renaissance, as, indeed, at any other time. The masculine frustration at not being biologically capable of developing and delivering a human being corresponds to the much-vaunted 'female penis-envy'. What woman lacks in external and visible machinery, however, man lacks on the inside. The female's inward and mysterious nature, her kinship with cats, her lunar emotionality, are all referrable to that inner mechanism, the invisible 'o' where conception occurs and pregnancy proceeds. Even as woman may yearn to own the masculine, rodlike 'I', shedder of seed, so does the man subconsciously contemplate the womb.

Thomas Raynalde's *The Byrth of Mankynde, otherwyse named The Womans Booke* (1560) expresses a view of woman's superior generative powers in a way that might well provoke masculine insecurity: in woman, says Raynalde,

> truely is the receptacle, and as ye woulde say, the campe or fielde of mankynde to be engendred therein. And although that man be as principall mover and cause of the generation, yet (no displeasure to men) the woman doth conferre and contribute much more. . . . And doubtlesse, yf a man woulde demaunde to whom the chylde oweth most his generation, ye may worthely make aunswere that, to the mother.[16]

This mid-century rational statement counterpoints the misogyny typified by John Knox's *Monstrous Regiment of Women* (1548).

Such theories filtered into *belles letters* via neo-Platonic thought, which recognised two routes to immortality: through one's child or through one's art. Indeed, the metaphor of generation affords an essential outlet for unconscious or repressed feminine elements in the masculine psyche. An archetypal fantasy recently identified as 'male motherhood of authorship'[17] permits man to accomplish in theory what he cannot in fact do: get pregnant and give birth. The progeny which crowns his travail is literary, and the readership upholds the good jest by referring to the *body* of a book.[18] The masculine need to partake directly in birth processes ensures the survival of generation metaphor, which is itself flexible enough to accommodate changing sexual or social values: the image of book-as-human-being, begot by male mother, persists to the present day.[19]

This enduring metaphor, simultaneously topical and classical, provides the prime means of self-expression for Renaissance writers. Pregnancy of imagination is the poet's ideal, and travail of childbirth the natural metaphor for poetic agony. Starting *Astrophel and Stella* (1591), Sidney finds himself 'great with Childe to speak',[20] and Chapman, dedicating *Achilles' Shield* (1598), describes how his soul's 'genuine forms struggle for birth'.[21] The same image appears in several prologues and letters dedicatory with the poet conventionally disclaiming fruitfulness. George Turberville writes to the reader with becoming modesty (1567): 'Here have I . . . given thee a few Sonets, the unripe seedes of my barraine braine.'[22] Likewise George Whetstone, to 'all the young Gentlemen of England' who may read his *Rocke of Regard* (1576), dismissing it as 'the first increase of my baren brain'.[23] In the dedication to his posthumously published *Arcadia* (1590), Sidney blushingly lets loose upon the world 'this child, which I am loath to father'.[24] The image often indicated parental pride, as in Spenser's exhortation to the newly delivered *Shepheardes Calender* (1579): 'Goe little booke: thy selfe present / As child whose parent is unkent.'[25]

Born from the poet's laborious throes, a new book was viewed as a vulnerable, helpless infant struggling for existence in an unfriendly world. Authors and printers alike emphasised the benign, fostering influence of patrons, a function implied by the etymological relationship between *patron* and Latin *pater*, 'father'. Blunt prefaced Marlowe's posthumously published *Hero and Leander* (1598) with this elaborate compliment to Sir Thomas Walsingham:

> I cannot but see so far into the will of him dead, that whatsoever issue of his brain should chance to come abroad, that the first breath it should take might be the gentle aire of your liking: for since his selfe had been accustomed thereunto, it would proove more agreeable and thriving to his right children than any other foster countenance whatsoever.[26]

Thomas Dekker presents *Newes From Hell* (1606) to 'my most respected, loving, and Juditious friend Mr. John Sturman Gentleman' as a brainchild sorely needing protection and patronage:

> Sir, the begetting of Bookes, is as common as the begetting of Children; onely heerein they differ, that Bookes speake so soone as they come into the world, and give the best wordes they can to al men, yet are they driven to seek abroad for a father. That hard fortune follows al & fals now upon THIS of mine. It gladly comes to you upon that errand, and if you vouchsafe to receive it lovingly, I shall account my selfe and it, very happie.[27]

More than the patron, the entire literary public was appealed to as a collective parent and charged with the nurture of the infant book. Florid obstetrical metaphors directed to the gentle and courteous reader begged his sympathetic response, often drawing attention to the manhandling that the poor 'baby' had suffered prior to release. Thomas Walkley refers to such abuses, incurred during printing, in his preface to the 1622 edition of Beaumont and Fletcher's *Philaster*:

> *Philaster* and *Arethusa*, his love, have laine so long a bleeding, by reason of some dangerous and gaping wounds which they received in the first Impression . . . maimed and deformed . . . they will now find double favour being reformed, and set forth suteable to their birth and breeding.[28]

Dekker alludes to post-publication injury of more subtle nature when prefacing *The Whore of Babylon* (1607), attempting to forestall wilful misunderstanding on the reader's part which could prove deformative to his brainchild:

> The labours . . . of Writers are as unhappie as the children of a bewtifull Woman, being spoyld by ill nurses, within a month after they come into the world. What a number of throwes do we endure eare we be delivered? And yet even then (tho that heavenly issue of our braine be never so faire and so well lymd), it is made lame by the bad handling of them to whom it is put to learne to goe: if this of mine be made a cripple by such meanes, yet dispise him not for that deformity which struck not upon him at his birth; but fell upon him by mis-fortune, and in recompence of such favour, you shall (if your Patience can suffer so long) heare now how himself can speake.[29]

The midwifely office of the printer helping the book to a successful birth is highlighted in Henry Olney's remarkable preface to Sidney's *An Apologie for Poetrie* (1595), whose coruscating imagery brings fully home to the audience their collective responsibility for the book's fate:

> The stormie Winter (deere Chyldren of the Muses) which hath so long held backe the glorious Sun-shine of divine Poesie, is heere by the sacred pen-breathing words of divine Sir *Phillip Sidney* not

onely chased from our fame-inviting Clyme, but utterly for ever banisht eternitie. Then graciously regreet the perpetuall spring of ever-growing invention, and like kinde Babes, either enabled by wit or power, help to support me poore Midwife, whose daring adventure hath delivered from Oblivions wombe this ever-to-be-admired wits miracle.[30]

The literary community, brotherhood of poets, is seen as the Muses' offspring, helping the printer to introduce a new child into their circle. Thus the Printer pleads for Greene's *Groatsworth of Wit* (1592): 'Accept it favourably because it was his last birth', using a metaphor of generation which Greene himself expands in his pathetic words: 'I commend this to your favourable censures, that like an Embrion without shape, I feare me will be thrust into the world.'[31]

Writers did not spare their audience any description of their prenatal pain. John Lyly gives a witty but none the less revealing account of monosexual literary parenthood in his preface to *Euphues and his England* (1580; repr. 1606), dedicated, significantly enough, to Edward de Vere, Earl of Oxford. Lyly describes his labour pains, confessing that 'the paine I sustained for him in travaile, hath made me past teeming, yet doe I think my self very fertile, in that I was not altogether barren'. Of this book's relationship with his first he asserts, 'Twinnes they are not, but yet brothers, the one nothing resembling the other, and yet as all children are now-a-daies, resembling the Father.'[32] Even more spectacular is Antony Scoloker's preface to *Daiphantus* (1604), where Daiphantus functions as persona to describe Scoloker's literary birth-throes:

> Passionate *Daiphantus*: Your loving Subject, Gives you to understand, He is *A man in Print*, and tis enough he hath under-gone a *Pressing* (yet not like a *Ladie*) though for your sakes and for *ladyes*, protesting for this poore Infant of his Brayne, as it was the price of his Virginitie borne into the world in tears . . .[33]

The metaphor of generation, which helped to usher the infant book into a waiting world, served also to register artistic displeasure and contempt among authors. Sidney's *Apologie* complains that it is 'now as if all the Muses were gotte with childe, to bring forth bastard Poets',[34] and Spenser scorns those poetasters who, 'being in the middest of all their bravery, sodenly, eyther for want of matter or of ryme, or having forgotten theyr former conceipt . . . seem to be so pained and traveiled in theyr remembrance, as it were a woman in childebirth'.[35] All this carping, however, pales before the great Harvey–Nashe conflict, whose prose, purple as anyone could wish, is enlivened by savage metaphors of generation used with blistering sarcasm by both parties to ridicule each other's aesthetic claims. Harvey writes,

> The difference of wittes is exceeding straung and almost incredible. Good lord, how may one man passe a thousand, and a thousande not compare with one? Arte may give out precepts and directoryes . . . but it is superexcellent witt that is the mother pearle of precious Invention, and the goulden mine of gorgeous Elocution. Na, it is a certaine pregnant and lively thing without name, but a queint mistery of mounting conceit, as it were a knacke of dexterity, or the nippitaty of the nappiest grape, that . . . will bunge Demosthenes owne mouth with new-fangled figures of the right stampe.[36]

Note the unmistakable physical suggestions surrounding 'pregnant': 'lively'= 'alive'; 'thing without name' connotes 'nothing' (= vagina); 'queint' = 'cunt'; 'mistery' connotes prostitution; 'mounting' is obscenely double-edged; and 'conceit' recalls the cognate 'conception'.

These vindictive innuendoes expressed Harvey's keenest scorn for Nashe's modern, pregnant 'Nature', which, lacking experience, sought to overturn the tried and tested 'Art' of the ancients. He inveighs against Nashe's 'brothell Muse'[37] and cautions that 'Pregnant Rules avail much, but visible Examples amount incredibly.'[38] He disgustedly recalls without naming 'the party, that in comparison of his owne naturall Inventions termed Pliny a barraine woombe',[39] and observes,

> It is for Cheeke or Ascham to stand levelling of Colons, or squaring of Periods, by measure and number: his [Nashe's] pen is like a spigot, and the Wine presse a dullard to his Ink-presse. There is a certain lively and frisking thing of a queint and capricious nature, as peerlesse as nameless, and as admirable as singular, that scorneth to be a book-worme, or to imitate the excellentest artificiality of the most renowned worke-masters that antiquity affourdeth. The witt of this and that odd Modernist is

their owne; & no such minerall of richest Art as praegnant Nature, the plentifullest woombe of rare Invention, and exquisite Elocution.[40]

Nashe replied in much the same terms, playing upon the metaphor of generation with predictable perversity. He ridiculed the 'excrementall conceipts'[41] of the Harvey brothers, and turned the generation metaphor against his enemies:

> Such is this golden age wherein we live, and so replenished with golden asses of all sortes, that, if learning had lost itselfe in a grove of Genealogies, we neede doe no more but sette an olde goose over half a dozen pottle pots (which are as it were the egges of invention) and wee shall have such a breede of bookes within a little while after, as will fill all the world with the wilde fowle of good wits.[42]

The ubiquitous metaphor of generation in these contexts establishes a 'pregnant poetic' for the Renaissance, an artistic convention which, though not as 'official' as Petrarchanism, none the less constituted an important, almost mandatory, literary element. It appears with astounding regularity, a wave of figurative pregnancy partly attributable to the novelty of popular printing and the great increase in publishing of literary texts. A book, after all, is not merely an object, but a subject (with its own *spine*). The metaphor, though broadly applied, was never rigidly schematised, and local usages conform only to the precise artistic nuance required. Sometimes the muses are pregnant, sometimes the poets. Sometimes imagination is fecund, sometimes poetic matter carries its own natal potential. Patrons may be foster-parents, and publishers midwives. Poetry itself may be either mother or offspring, and is variously seen as sister to eloquence or music. But, with all the inconsistency and variation, the Renaissance got under way and proceeded throughout the sixteenth century in enormous parturitive bursts.

The word 'pregnant' renders the metaphor of generation especially extravagant, but, though in the vanguard of the poetic effort, it rarely occurs with its explicit meaning the same as the modern literal sense 'with child'. Contextual vocabulary establishes that this significance was certainly implied. Why was the term not used in its obstetrical sense? Partly, probably, because of the tendency, still observable in contemporary medical prose, to

employ periphrastic and euphemistic terminology. Raynalde, our
mid-century 'phisition', delicately broaches his subject with the
cautious 'we will somwhat commune of conception'.[43]

Substance (the tangible end product) is the common de-
nominator between the poets, who fancied themselves 'pregnant',
and the physician Raynalde, who mulls over poetic methods and
the problems of inspiration in the prologue to his enormously
popular obstetrical handbook:

> the auncyente Poetes in tymes passyd, when that they en-
> terprysed anye newe or straunge workes, were wont in the frunt of
> the same, with great protestation, to invocate and call upon all
> the goddes and goddesses by name. . .
>
> Whose example, ryght necessary and nedeful it were that I
> here should full devoutely ensue and folowe. . . . But truely I do
> suppose that although I should call downe all the .ix. noble
> Muses [he names other medicinal and witty deities] . . . in whom
> ingenious Poetes do fayne to be a majestie, might and
> power. . . with their holy poetical spirite to breathe over this
> boke, yet should there be founde people . . . that woulde
> (without all good reason) blame.[44]

He rejects the idea of commandeering the poet's idiom.

But, sharing the obstetrician's language, the poets laboured on
undeterred. Consider the forces at work behind Alexander Barclay's
Prologue to *Certayne Egloges* (*c.* 1514, published 1570):

> The famous Poetes with the Muses nine,
> With wit inspired, fresh, pregnant, and divine,
> Say, boldly indite in stile substanciall.[45]

This self-congratulation is ridiculed in Thomas Wilson's *Arte of
Rhetorique* (1553), where, in a parodic model letter, a writer
flourishes to his patron: 'how could you have adepted such illustrate
prerogative, and dominicall superioritee, if the fecunditee of your
ingenie had not been so fertile, and wonderful pregnant?'[46]

If the pregnant poetic seemed laughable to Wilson, it was a
matter of extreme seriousness to the anonymous author of *Zepheria*
(1594), who claims immortality as the reward of poetic labour for
his colleagues, the *veri figlioli delle Muse* ('true-born little sons of the
Muses'):

> Ye modern Lawreats, famousd for your writ,
> Who for your pregnance may in Delos dwell,
> On your sweete lines eternitie doth sit,
> Their browes enobling with applause and lawrell.[47]

With the mention of that eternity attendant on truly substantial verse, let us turn our attention to Shakespeare, the most pregnant poet of the period. Dedicated to W. H., their 'onlie begetter', and promising 'eternity', the *Sonnets* (*c.* 1593–6, published 1609) grew out of the Renaissance pregnant poetic, but displayed an important difference. Shakespeare assumed the poet's conventional power to recreate and eternise the Beloved through his art, but he went one stage further in urging his lover to procreate his own image by having a real child as well:

> From fairest creatures we desire increase,
> That thereby beauty's rose might never die . . .
>
> (i. 1–2)

> Unthrifty loveliness, why dost thou spend
> Upon thyself thy beauty's legacy?
> Nature's bequest gives nothing, but doth lend,
> And, being frank, she lends to those are free.
>
> (iv. 1–4)

> And nothing 'gainst Time's scythe can make defence
> Save breed, to brave him when he takes thee hence.
>
> (xii. 13–14)

Venus uses an identical argument in her attempted seduction of Adonis (*Venus and Adonis*, 1593):

> Seeds spring from seeds and beauty breedeth beauty;
> Thou wast begot; to get it is thy duty.

> Upon the earth's increase why shouldst thou feed,
> Unless the earth with thy increase be fed?
> By law of nature thou art bound to breed,
> That thine may live when thou thyself art dead;
> And so, in spite of death, thou dost survive,
> In that thy likeness still is left alive.
>
> (ll. 167–74)

The arguments for actual procreation advanced by Venus and by Shakespeare's persona in the *Sonnets* generate central points of conflict. The artistic ideal – pregnancy – becomes literal.

At the same time, Shakespeare shared with his peers the view of poetic product as child. He had described *Venus and Adonis* as 'the first heir of my invention', but not until the *Sonnets* does his pride of literary paternity become fully apparent, as in Sonnet lxxvi:

> Why is my verse so barren of new pride,
> So far from variation or quick change?
> Why with the time do I not glance aside
> To new-found methods and to compounds strange?
> Why write I still all one, ever the same,
> And keep invention in a noted weed,
> That every word doth almost tell my name,
> Showing their birth and where they did proceed?
> O, know, sweet love, I only write of you . . . .
>
> (ll. 1–9)

Shakespeare rightly identified the ground of his individuality: the delicate subject of his verse – his masculine friend – pitched his poems into regions virtually unexplored by other Elizabethan poets. One of the birthmarks of his sonnet-cycle was the double creativity which I have just defined, a fusion of actual and metaphorical generation. This simultaneity manifests itself in Sonnet xvii, which suggests that the physical presence of his lover's child would substantiate the compliments in Shakespeare's poetry for sceptical future readers, and provide double indemnity against annihilation:

> were some child of yours alive that time,
> You should live twice, in it and in my rhyme.
>
> (ll. 13–14)

Creativity in the *Sonnets*, then, is both literal and metaphorical, and advances beyond the Elizabethan figurative pregnancy of the poet. Shakespeare's spirit of creativity embraces not only author but also subject.

The conceptions, or conceits, of Elizabethan writers are the preconceptions from which Shakespeare's dramatic art evolved. He successfully transferred the generation metaphor to dramatic contexts, developing the primary life-metaphor of his early poetry in character, structure, plot and theme. Oddly enough, no full-length study has been devoted to the incidence of pregnancy in Shakespeare's plays, and its implications for Shakespeare's creative method or the enduring and universal appeal of his work. But its importance cannot be underestimated, and its nature demands investigation. It is precisely because Shakespeare's characters partake of the very stuff of life that they seem so real. In Iago's declaration 'My Muse labours,/And thus she is delivered' (*Othello*, II. i. 128–9), we can discern a creative process identical with Shakespeare's own: the human mind conceiving a brainchild. Iago himself, however, is Shakespeare's mental offspring. Shakespeare allowed his literary creations their own power of creativity; like duplicating cells, the creativity multiplies and spreads, inevitably touching audience, reader and actor.

The process of literary creation involves the expression of a content in some suitable form, or, as New Criticism would have it, a *tenor* conveyed through some *vehicle*. In Iago's speech, just quoted, the tenor is, 'I am trying hard to come up with a poem, and have succeeded.' His vehicle is a metaphor of generation: the labouring Muse. The early emphasis of Shakespeare's *Sonnets* (before the Dark Lady appears) is on tenor, with the message 'My love, you owe it to the world to have a child.' The literal child becomes part of a vehicular generation metaphor as the *Sonnets* progress, conveying a new message: 'My poems (are children that) will eternise you.' In Shakespeare's drama, the shift takes the reverse direction. Metaphor (vehicle) of the early plays becomes the dramatic world (tenor) which informs the later plays. To state this theory another way: the early events on the brain-stage develop into events on the world-stage. Modes of perception and cognition for the early characters develop into lifestyles and environments for protagonists of Shakespeare's mature and late works: Romeo has a bad dream; Hermione *is* Leontes's bad dream.[48]

Of course, such distinctions are largely artificial, incapable of defence, and, for the intelligent reader, faintly insidious. Not for one moment do we believe that Shakespeare sat down to write saying, 'I am going to do such-and-such with pregnancy this time.' During Shakespeare's career, and at almost any stage of it, boundaries between form and content continually and imperceptibly dissolve. The drama occurs on some indefinable middle ground, where language, symbol, and event intermingle. Abstract and concrete coalesce, as is reflected in the title of a recent study of Shakespearian dream: *From Metaphor to Metamorphosis*.[49] Most interpreters of Shakespeare's work agree on his increasing fusion of literal and figurative dramatic elements, the mysterious homogeneity towards which he tends. Shakespeare proceeds 'from the purely decorative to the functional image',[50] so that finally 'the plot has become simply an extension, an extra vehicle of the poetry'.[51]

In following Shakespeare's development of the generation metaphor, we shall see the same broad trends operating. We shall examine a few plays from each of his artistic periods: lyrical, problematic, tragic and romantic. In the early plays, particularly those lyrical dramas where Shakespeare developed his poetic style, the generation metaphor defines thought-process and imagination along lines similar to the Renaissance pregnant poetic. Even at the lyrical stage, however, Shakespeare subtly reins in his metaphor to reflect the large themes of each play. The problem plays gradually literalise the generation metaphor, exploring man's fertile state and supporting their more frankly erotic plots with fertility imagery and wordplay. In the tragedies, despite the keynote of death, the generation metaphor is fully established as verbal and thematic underpinning, defining and measuring man's physical and mental creativity. The romances fuse literal and figurative fertility in actual regeneration, expressed in verbal and visual metaphors of generation which cumulatively exert powerful thematic and dramatic influence. Major fertility symbols of the last plays will be recognised as expanded versions of those images which Shakespeare habitually associates with womanhood and birth. The regenerative thrust of the romances will not indicate merely a vague satiation with tragic writing on Shakespeare's part. There is a definite moment which signals the end of Shakespeare's tragic development and which turns him toward romance and rebirth. As we shall also see, the romances put Shakespeare's entire dramatic output in perspective and represent the final evolutionary stage in his development of generation metaphor.

While the figurative-to-literal development is pretty clear, it should not be too dogmatically insisted upon. One might expect that over a twenty-year period a writer's view of generation would undergo considerable change, according to the influence of his experiences; that what is a gleam in the father's eye in 1595 becomes living generation by 1613. Between Richard II's intellectual exercise of making fruitful marriages in his head and the triumphal rebirths of the romances, the generation metaphor appears in many guises: as a linguistic feature (in pun and wordplay), as visual image (icon, stage, or situational), as plot or theme, and as itself – metaphor for mental action. This last was probably Shakespeare's most characteristic and best-loved correspondence, typifying his creative genius. His wit encompasses both spiritual values and below-the-belt bawdy; his generation metaphor, which speaks of brain or belly, neatly bridges both worlds.

Generation, while surely the supreme index of creativity, is not the only one; nor is it, despite its primacy, the only creative language to which Shakespeare tunes his verse.[52] But it is the most important one, and a force which shapes our reactions to his drama. Not only does the metaphor of generation indicate Shakespeare's creative worldview, it also dramatically awakens in us our own grandest possibilities with a universality that demands empathy, and which is the quintessence of living theatre. Shakespeare's creativity is most powerfully evident in his primary metaphor of creativity, sympathetically echoed in the appreciative vocabulary of countless critics since the posthumous publication of the First Folio in 1623. Describing their editorial function, Heminge and Condell compared the plays to orphans:

> since your L.L. [lordships] have been pleas'd to thinke these trifles some-thing, heeretofore; and have prosequuted both them, and their Authour living, with so much favour: we hope, that (they out-living him, and he not having the fate, common with some, to be exequutor to his owne writings) you will use the like indulgence toward them, you have done unto their parent. There is a great difference, whether any Booke choose his Patrones, or finde them: This hath done both. For, so much were your L.L. likings of the severall parts, when they were acted, as before they were published, the Volume ask'd to be yours. We have but collected them, and done an office to the dead, to procure his Orphanes, Guardians . . . we most humbly consecrate to your H.H. [highnesses] these remaines of your servant SHAKESPEARE. . .[53]

2 'Conceit's Expositor': The Lyrical Plays

Shakespeare's four great plays of *c.* 1595–6, *Romeo and Juliet*, *A Midsummer Night's Dream*, *Richard II* and *Love's Labour's Lost*, span comic, historic and tragic genres; but, despite their generic incompatibility, they share a major poetic trait. In all these plays, Shakespeare works out the plot or theme in polarisations of light/dark, sun/moon, ear/eye, man/animal, reason/imagination, beauty/grotesque, and so on, which fulfil the double function of honing his poetic art to a fine point and of establishing the poetic values upon which his succeeding drama is based. These schoolboy contrasts, coupled with the verse's vernal character, bespeak a lyrical stage of development. In this period, Shakespeare begins fully to realise his poetic powers, already apparent in the embryonic art of *Titus Andronicus*, *The Comedy of Errors* and *Henry VI*.[1] Here he learns, like Biron (or Berowne), to discipline his freewheeling fancy: to be an apt expositor of his conceits. Although a delighted air of linguistic experiment persists, Shakespeare starts to direct his imagery and wordplay toward the larger thematic aim of the plays, so that the imagery becomes altogether more sophisticated: lying closer to the heart of the plot, less gratuitous, more thematically weighted.

In the lyrical plays, the metaphor of generation, traversing generic boundaries, fittingly expresses the re-creative ability of Shakespeare's protagonists, defining and describing the human thought or action process. Optical and auditory errors strike their sense, excite the imagination, and emerge as re-created reality. Not seeing straight, nor hearing right, the characters fashion alternative universes in their personal quest for truth. Even when the metaphor apparently is restricted to a single speech, its influence permeates the play in which it occurs, providing a creative context for the developing drama.

Mercutio is a marvellous example of these radiating significances.

His witty verbal fencing has elicited description of him as 'Romeo's loquacious friend', while his Queen Mab speech (I. iv. 53–94) has been variously seen as an interpolation, a 'display aria', an 'anatomy of self-deception'. Along with the Nurse, Mercutio is classed as 'the most fertile of storytellers'.[2] The adjective is appropriate, since the Nurse's reminiscence (I. ii. 16–48) closes with a prophecy that Juliet will fall upon her back when she attains sexual maturity, and Mercutio's speech is interrupted after he hints at what befalls girls who lie on their backs.

The Queen Mab speech uses pun and folklore to establish generation as the defining metaphor for human imagination. It has three movements:[3] lines 54–69 identify Mab as the fairies' midwife and describe her chariot; lines 70–88 enumerate the wish-fulfilment dreams which she creates during her rapid nocturnal progress; and lines 88–94 hint darkly at mischief, horsehair and pregnancy. These last six lines have received scant editorial attention, and a closer look at them may reveal why. Despite all the appearances of gossamer diversion, the Mab speech, with its strong undercurrents of sex and generation, fittingly supports the tragic prematurity theme and ominously foreshadows the death of Mercutio.

Mab herself is mythologically related to the Celtic fertility deities Medb (or Maeve), Rhiannon and Macha. They are all linked to bull and horse figures, which symbolise fertility. Jobes instances a legend where Medb won and kept the Brown Bull of Ulster (fertility) after a battle which Cuchulainn (the sun) fought in single combat against her whole army (darkness), and she is usually interpreted as 'a moon goddess or queen of darkness'.[4] In Shakespeare, sexual intercourse is typically associated with darkness. Regarding Epona, the original deity from whom these goddesses derive, we learn that 'the horse goddess emerges as another manifestation of the mother goddess'.[5] And Mab's carriage is horse-drawn.

Mab's mythological descent ensures that the act will be procreative as well as libidinous. Her midwifely function is also reflected in her name, Welsh for 'baby' or 'child'. Gertrude Jobes interprets Mab as 'a midwife to men's fancies, i.e., she delivers men's brains of dreams'.[6] This is only partly true. Mab does start out in the brain, but she ends up in the genitals. The last portion of Mercutio's speech, which concentrates on her malign sexuality, is designedly emphatic. In order that no folkloric association be lost, Mercutio prefaces his last remarks insistently and with a decidedly unlyrical

'This is . . . this is . . . this is . . . . ' To borrow his phrase, this is a far cry from the elegant lyricism of the opening: '*she is* the fairies' midwife'. Mercutio weaves incantatory magic into his delineation of her entourage; but Mab's progress brings hypocrisy, disease, avarice, sharp legal and ecclesiastical practice, and murder to the minds of her dreamers. And, finally, the fairy queen is horribly transformed:

> *This is that very Mab*
> That plats the manes of horses in the night,
> And bakes the elf-locks in foul sluttish hairs,
> Which, once untangled, much misfortune bodes.
> *This is the hag*, when maids lie on their backs,
> That presses them and learns them first to bear,
> Making them women of good carriage.
> *This is she* –

(1. iv. 88–95, emphasis added)

From the fragile little spirit in her nutshell coach, we have moved with Mercutio through 'angry Mab', arriving at 'the hag'. Mercutio ends, brilliantly, where he started, on the word 'she'; but with what alteration!

Mab's attack on horses places her in the tradition of the nightmare. The horsehair which she so assiduously plaits is, of course, human female pubic hair,[7] a reading easily justified by recalling the Renaissance slang use of 'jade' for 'prostitute', not to mention the many *double entendres* in Shakespeare where horse and woman are linked. Of these possibly the most notorious, certainly the most extended, is the discussion between the Dauphin and his court on skill in 'horsemanship' ('whoresmanship') in *Henry V*, III. vii.[8] The untangling of these hairs certainly does bode misfortune: in folklore, knotted hair is a protective charm for virgins.[9] Once pubic hair is unknotted, penetration is easier. The creative dream actualises in procreation. Mab sits suffocatingly on her victim,[10] causing erotic fantasies which fulfil themselves in actual pregnancy.

Mercutio's speech occurs in the scene before Romeo and Juliet first meet. Inevitably, Romeo interrupts Mercutio here. Romeo's is the innocent voice of the adolescent in an adolescent play whose lyrical universe is not yet old enough to handle the gritty adult realities which Mercutio describes.[11] The sight of Juliet on her balcony recalls the eastern, dawning sun. Later for Shakespeare, much later, a beautiful woman – Cleopatra – will shine like the 'eastern star' (representing evening) at the moment of her death, while she suckles the deadly asp. In *Romeo and Juliet*, however, the breastfeeding imagery of Nurse and Friar[12] denotes a young, pubescent world, which cannot sustain Mercutio. The connection between Mercutio's verbal and physical fencing is tragic: Romeo's second restraint of Mercutio comes not in conversation, but in action, after his marriage to Juliet, and results in Mercutio's death.

For the moment, however, Mercutio has an alternative. He withdraws from the physical forum, converting the gross reality he has depicted into metaphor:

> ROMEO. Peace, peace, Mercutio, peace!
>   Thou talk'st of nothing.
> MERCUTIO. True, I talk of dreams,
> Which are the children of an idle brain,
> Begot of nothing but vain fantasy,
> Which is as thin of substance as the air
> And more inconstant than the wind . . .

(I. iv. 95–100)

Mercutio's metaphor takes up right where he left off: at pregnancy. Only, this time, the real pregnancy is upwardly displaced back to the brain, where it becomes the figurative birth of the wild nocturnal imagination.[13]

Eric Partridge was on the right track when, interpreting Shakespeare's bawdy, he remarked, 'To write is, in fact, to create; and to make love is potentially to create.' He concluded that for Shakespeare 'composition is superior to love-making as a means of satisfying the need for self-expression (or "the creative urge")'.[14] This implies much about what Shakespeare felt for his plays, but it ignores his relationship with his characters. Certainly, Shakespeare revelled in the knowledge of his creative powers. I would further contend that he transferred this creativity to almost all his characters, in that they also can generate and give birth to thoughts as well as to children. All humans can think; what matters is *how* they think. The uniqueness and the accessibility of Shakespeare's characters lies in their creativity, characteristically conveyed in the language of pregnancy. Their continual concern with clear perception and right nomination ('what's in a name?') evidences a constant creative process, most forcefully expressed when these themes are wedded to generation metaphor.

The erring nocturnal imagination, prey to the subconscious, whose inner eye creates distorted visions, provides the theme and plot of *A Midsummer Night's Dream*. As in *Romeo and Juliet*, the dream experience is related to childbirth,[15] but its development takes a different form, relying on more strongly motivated optical imagery, and offering a more hopeful view of the regenerative power of dream. So, whereas Mercutio passes off dreams as 'more inconstant than the wind', the more tolerant Hippolyta finds in them 'something of great constancy' (v. i. 26). Puck gives more positive reinforcement to Mercutio's damning 'children of an idle brain' with his easygoing defence of 'this weak and idle theme' (v. i. 434). Even the nightmarish horses are comically transmuted into Bottom-with-an-ass's-head. This optimism also manifests itself in a comic reversal of the dramatic priorities of *Romeo and Juliet*. The Queen Mab speech is a pre-party episode in a double-suicide plot. However, echoes of the dream resound throughout *Romeo and Juliet* and move beneath its structure like a groundswell. In *A Midsummer Night's Dream*, the dream is absolutely central to the drama, and *Pyramus and Thisbe* – the double-suicide play – is relegated to the status of after-dinner entertainment, although, again, the minor string vibrates powerfully. The artisans' production of *Pyramus and Thisbe* runs beneath the play with its own current. In *Romeo and Juliet*, then, we view reality against the backdrop of dream. In *A Midsummer Night's Dream*' we see dream against the attempt to make dream real. The fertility symbols traditionally associated with Mab, all part of the substructure of *Romeo and Juliet*, move to the foreground in *A Midsummer Night's Dream*.

The creative spirit is apparent in Oberon's intent to bless the marriage of Theseus and Hippolyta. Unfortunately, a quarrel with his wife, Titania, delays him. Their marital spat has produced a terrible 'baby' – chaos in nature – for whom Titania assumes parental responsibility:

> the spring, the summer,
> The childing autumn, angry winter, change
> Their wonted liveries; and the mazed world,
> By their increase, now knows not which is which.
> And this same progeny of evils comes

From our debate, from our dissension;
We are their parents and original.[16]

(II. i. 111–17)

The language of parenthood fits the occasion, since Oberon and
Titania are disputing each other's claim to custody of an orphan
boy. Titania graphically recalls his mother's expectancy in robust,
fertile language:

His mother was a vot'ress of my order,
And, in the spiced Indian air, by night,
Full often hath she gossip'd by my side,
And sat with me on Neptune's yellow sands,
Marking th'embarked traders on the flood,
When we have laugh'd to see the sails conceive
And grow big-bellied with the wanton wind;
Which she with pretty and with swimming gait
Following, her womb then rich with my young squire,
Would imitate, and sail upon the land
To fetch me trifles, and return again,
As from a voyage, rich with merchandise.

(II. i. 123–34)

Titania's recollections exhibit her frank eroticism and healthy joy in
maternity. Hurling defiance in Oberon's teeth, she walks off with
the child. Oberon complements her dreamlike, symbolic narrative
with one of his own, in language which betrays repressed and
unproductive phallicism. He recalls sitting one cold night on a
promontory, watching a singing mermaid ride a dolphin; the stars
shot orgasmically in response. Oberon's super-priapic vision of
armed Cupid missing a virgin and deflowering a flower with his
'love-shaft' (II. i. 159) was not shared by Puck ('I saw, but thou
couldst not' – II. i. 155). In polar opposition to Titania, who stresses
warmth, companionship, womb symbols, pregnancy, Oberon
dwells on coldness, solitude, phallic symbols, the masturbatory
thrill of the voyeur. In contrast to Titania's rosy recall of her gravid
votaress, who seemed to swim, shiplike,[17] so leisurely along the land,
Puck, proud of his speed in girdling the earth, is ordered by Oberon
to return 'ere the leviathan can swim a league' (II. i. 174).
  These traumatic echoes reveal that the quarrel between Titania

and Oberon touches ancient and primitive human sexual jealousies, epitomising the basic psychological and biological differences between male and female; Oberon avenges himself by initiating figurative counterparts to the pregnancy Titania described. He uses the very flower whose defloration ('before milk-white, now purple with love's wound' – II. i. 167) he witnessed, and, voyeuristically enough, aims his revenge at the eye – the main gate to the creative faculty. The flower is Pansy; the etymological relationship of its name with *pensée* identifies it as the herb of creating thought.[18] Under its magic influence, and further confused by the New Moon phase, when 'the brain is not so fully obedient to the spirit of feeling'[19] as usual, the dreamers recreate new and monstrous realities. Their creativity is explicitly connected with sight, since Oberon's remedy is empowered to make their 'eyeballs roll with wonted sight' so that 'When they next wake, all this derision / Shall seem a dream and fruitless vision' (III. ii. 370–1). Even after the awakening, Theseus compares the fruitful coining of the 'lunatic' brain to the generative action of poetic imagination, also set in train by the eye, which,

> in a fine frenzy rolling,
> Doth glance from heaven to earth, from earth to heaven;
> And as imagination bodies forth
> The forms of things unknown, the poet's pen
> Turns them to shapes and gives to airy nothing
> A local habitation and a name.

(v. i. 12–17)

Theseus equates the lover, the lunatic and the poet, linking them through the metaphor of generation. Titania and Oberon represent the theme of actual generation; the dreamers' mad recreation, their eyes impregnated with error and fantasy, provides figurative generation. Now Theseus discusses that poetic creativity which brings forth brainchildren, capable of identification: the creativity of the master mind behind *A Midsummer Night's Dream* itself, and which burlesques its own activity in *Pyramus and Thisbe*.

Itself a 'creation', *Pyramus and Thisbe* has substance only if the inner eye of the imagination will do its supplementary work and 'amend' the limitations of theatre. Shakespeare fully develops this idea in *Henry V*, where the Chorus exhorts the audience to fill the theatre's 'o' with their creative imaginations. The bringing forth of

Pyramus and Thisbe is an act of aesthetic generation, all the more so
since Puck writes the players off as 'that barren sort' (III. ii. 13), and
Philostrate scorns them as men who 'never labour'd in their minds
till now' (v. i. 73). The generative quality of play-making has
recently been described in these terms:

> To put it simply, birth is a creative act. We view the actor as
> basically performing functions of a receptive, feminine nature.
> The script is the father which impregnates him. The director is
> the midwife helping it along, tugging and coaxing the new born
> babe, the character, out.[20]

For Theseus, at least, the play has life: it is 'palpable-gross' (v. i. 374).

The conflicts of *A Midsummer Night's Dream* resolve in a finale
which anticipates the birth of children. The discord between
Oberon and Titania, prompted by a baby, dissolves in epithalamion, and the promise of 'fruitful, generative monogamy'.[21]
Indeed, parenthood may be the only means of keeping the naturally
antagonistic sexes from each other's throats and affording a tenuous
peace in their eternal battle, as this view suggests:

> Primal, eternal enemies, locked in forever, with no hope of
> escape. . . . Male and female trapped on the planet. At first they
> will engage in total war, since they are natural enemies. . . .
>
> The opposites, just *because* they are in conflict, will gradually draw
> together, and what looked like death and destruction will settle
> down into a latent state of concord, suitably expressed by the
> symbol of pregnancy. . . .
>
> The dawn of the new age is always symbolized by the birth of a
> child.[22]

During the epithalamion, Oberon moves the generation metaphor
into the sphere of reality: he blesses the eventual issue of the triple
marriage and re-emphasises the connection between generation
and vision with his curse on 'mark prodigious, such as are / Despised
in nativity' (v. i. 419–20). In terms of the relationship between
birthmarks and evil attributes of personality,[23] we may compare
Queen Margaret's curse on Richard III, whom she describes as
'Thou elvish-mark'd, abortive, rooting hog!' (*Richard III*, I. iii. 228).
The use of 'abortive' in this context is particularly interesting, since

Richard is incapable of creative action. Oberon's speech is designed to ward off such curses, and the optical sense, which is so important during *A Midsummer Night's Dream*, has its own special part to play in epithalamion.

Creativity in *A Midsummer Night's Dream* embraces actual generation, generation of thought, and generation of art. The episodes of failed or unhappy parenthood find their harmonious resolution in epithalamion; the shapes created by the dreamers' minds remain mercifully subconscious; we gain insight about aesthetic creation and audience responsibility from *Pyramus and Thisbe*. These three creative acts represent a progressive movement out of the body toward the spiritual realm. Puck asks our indulgence for *A Midsummer Night's Dream* in exactly the terms which Theseus uses to excuse *Pyramus and Thisbe*:

> THESEUS. The best in this kind are but shadows, and
> the worst are no worse, if imagination amend them.

(v. i. 213–14)

> ROBIN. If we shadows have offended,
> Think but this, and all is mended . . .

(v. i. 430–1)

Finally, then, the consummately creative act of mental generation belongs to the audience. Our amendment of the shadows embodied by our imaginations dictates our view and results in our own creation of reality.[24]

In both *Romeo and Juliet* and *A Midsummer Night's Dream*, the generative operation of imagination relates closely to the faculty of sight, an association iconographically depicted in schematic eye – brain diagrams of the Middle Ages. In these striking drawings, optic nerves connect the eyes with the brain.[25] For Shakespeare, this interconnectedness is a leading dramatic and thematic motif, and the eye plays a pre-eminent role in determining the character of thought. The commonplace notion of critics that illusion is the 'grand theme' of the comedies[26] finds paradigmatic utterance in the song commissioned by Portia for Bassanio, where the metaphor of generation describes the birth and death of fancy occuring in the eye:

> Tell me where is fancy bred,
> Or in the heart or in the head?

> How begot, how nourished?
> Reply, reply.
>
> It is engend'red in the eyes,
> With gazing fed; and fancy dies
> In the cradle where it lies.
> Let us all ring fancy's knell;
> I'll begin it, – Ding, dong, bell.
>
> > (*The Merchant of Venice*,
> > III. ii. 63–72)

Like distorting mirrors, tears further increase the general unreliability of sight. For instance, Lysander tearfully attests his newborn faith to the wrong woman: 'Look, when I vow, I weep; and vows so born, / In their nativity all truth appears' (III. ii. 124–5). Apparently not so. In the forest, everyone cries in confusion – the girls, the moon, even the flowerets in Bottom's crown.[27] On the other hand, tears shed in Athens are comedic: Philostrate cries with laughter at the thought of *Pyramus and Thisbe*, which, like its frame play, will ask 'tears in the true performing of it' (I. ii. 27–8).

Tears are watery, of course, and form part of the water-image which symbolically opposes sun-imagery in *A Midsummer Night's Dream*. Although it is impossible to legislate for all instances, we may generally observe the following polarities, typical of Shakespeare's lyrical period, whereby contrasting worlds in the play define themselves:

day	night
sun	moon
fire, air	earth, water
power of words	imperfection of visual perception
– sounds	– visions
strength	weakness
power	manipulability
invulnerability	vulnerability
action	imagination

These symbols occur in language or as stage images. Their dramatic operation may be seen in the morning arrival of Hippolyta and Theseus, who break the damp night's optical illusion and enter in bright sunlight to the blare of trumpets, full of auditory reminiscences.

The same vocabulary of symbols, representing confusion and clarity, is present in *Richard II*, and applies to the political, rather than to the emotional, struggle. For example, Henry Bolingbroke appropriates all the sunlike power of Richard's kingly word, leaving him threading the needle's eye and creating concepts in a watery world of tears.

The perceptual birth through the 'glass' of tears is an important motif in *Richard II*, and links the experiences of Richard and Isabel. Isabel, dreading the future, conceives a nameless woe in the form of 'some unborn sorrow, ripe in fortune's womb' (II. ii. 10). Bushy attempts to dispel her growing grief by arguing that she views the situation distortedly through the perspective glass of her tears, seeing the shadow only, and not the substance. In creating a complex multiplicity of images,[28] whether 'real' or not, the Queen labours under the physical sensation of a mother straining in childbirth:

> my inward soul
> With nothing trembles.
>
> (II. ii. 11–12)

> I cannot but be sad; so heavy sad
> As, though on thinking on no thought I think,
> Makes me with heavy nothing faint and shrink.
>
> (II. ii. 30–2)

Bushy dismisses her pain, far more accurately than he realises, as imaginary 'conceit' (II. ii. 33). Isabel picks up the literal sense of the cognate word 'concept' as she elaborates on the mysterious origins of her mental baby:

> conceit is still deriv'd
> From some forefather grief; mine is not so,
> For nothing hath begot my something grief,
> Or something hath the nothing that I grieve.
> 'Tis is reversion that I do possess;
> But what it is, that is not yet known; what,
> I cannot name; 'tis nameless woe, I wot.
>
> (II. ii. 34–40)

Eric La Guardia has recently observed that Isabel here replaces imagination with 'an attitude toward reality which excludes naming ("nameless woe"), but which nevertheless perceives a substantiality in "nothing"'.[29] To Isabel, nothing, being real in and of itself, needs neither word nor symbol to prove its existence.

Green's entrance helps to turn *nothing* into *something*, and effects Isabel's difficulty delivery of her thoughts. As he supplies the missing name – 'Bolingbroke' – she cries,

> So, Green, thou art the midwife to my woe,
> And Bolingbroke my sorrow's dismal heir.
> Now hath my soul brought forth her prodigy,
> And I, a gasping new-deliver'd mother,
> Have woe to woe, sorrow to sorrow join'd.

(II. ii. 62–6)

Eric La Guardia's study ignores this important 'birth speech' of Isabel's. More strangely, in contrasting Richard's absolute reliance on symbol and verbiage with Isabel's apparent indifference to the 'creative power of the word',[30] La Guardia skips straight to Richard's Pomfret soliloquy at the end of the play (v. v. 1–66), missing the crucial Westminster Hall scene (IV. i). This scene is of paramount importance in terms of structure and character development. Isabel's 'woe to woe, sorrow to sorrow join'd' makes sense only in light of her husband's parallel experience in Act IV scene i.

The Westminster Hall scene portrays the second of three mental births which occur in *Richard II*. All are associated with Bolingbroke, who is, in effect, the new baby fostered and nursed by Mother England, and, in a larger sense, by fate itself. Hence the numerous child-images surrounding Bolingbroke, who marvels at the growth of his 'infant fortune' (II. iii. 66), while appearing to Berkeley like one who comes to 'fright our native peace with self-born arms' (II. iii. 80, with a neat pun on *borne/born*). The end of the play shows Bolingbroke, in a typically Shakespearian conflation of vegetative and human growth images, regretting that 'blood should sprinkle me to make me grow' (v. vi. 46).[31]

The three births of the play take place before, during and after a historical fact – the 'fact' being the unstoppable rise of Bolingbroke. Shakespeare meticulously lays the dramatic ground for each birth before it happens. The John of Gaunt deathbed scene preceding

Isabel's mental pregnancy is replete with maternal images of national character: England is 'This happy breed of men . . . This nurse, this teeming womb of royal kings' (II. i. 45, 51). Gaunt descends to the grave, 'whose hollow womb inherits nought but bones' (II. i. 83). In symphonic[32] restatement, these images are transferred to the workings of Isabel's soul as she prophetically conceives historical reality.[33]

The idea of country-as-mother affords an appropriately fertile setting for Shakespeare's histories. Throughout these, whole countries are seen as good or bad mothers (this latter occasionally equalises with a view of country-as-whore), and their populations accordingly identified as true-born men or bastards. The rise of individual fortunes on the political scene is often marked in *Richard II*, and the histories in general, by images implicitly or explicitly associated with birth.

As the unnamable Bolingbroke emerges as a threat and gradually comes to dominate the political scene, Isabel makes her second appearance in the garden episode (III. iv), which prepares us for the second birth in the play. The Duke of York's garden, in which she stands, is a literalised and scaled-down version of Gaunt's Edenic garden of England. Those 'too fast growing sprays, / That look too lofty in our commonwealth' (III. iv. 34–5) will appear as traitors in Westminster Hall, clearly seen by a weeping Richard, in the next scene. And to prepare us for Richard's tears, the Queen weeps again, as the Gardener remarks:

> Here did she fall a tear; here in this place
> I'll set a bank of rue, sour herb of grace.
> Rue, even for ruth, here shortly shall be seen,
> In the remembrance of a weeping queen.
>
> (III. iv. 104–7)

That Shakespeare intended a similarity between the thought-processes of Richard and those of Isabel is certain, although the Queen's experiences are generally more physically immediate than Richard's. Isabel operates beyond the level of a weepy, pale queen drifting pathetically through the chaos,[34] and furnishes another powerful dramatic foil to Richard's character. He has merely contributed to the decay of the garden of England; she finds herself actually standing there.

The garden of England moves indoors to Westminster Hall, where Richard and Bolingbroke will confront each other. Bolingbroke, child of the time, is reborn as Richard's royal successor:

> Great Duke of Lancaster, I come to thee
> From plume-pluck'd Richard; who with willing soul
> Adopts thee heir . . .
>
> (IV. i. 107–9)

Richard enters to complete, ritualistically, his enforced adoption of Bolingbroke. Wishing the usurper power in the form of 'many years of sunshine days!' (IV. i. 221), Richard thinks to have finished his self-sacrifice. But the relinquishing of his kingly accoutrements does not satisfy Northumberland, who wishes Richard to acknowledge his inner impurity. Richard passes from sunshine to tears. Unable to read for weeping, he nevertheless distinctly sees – and names – the source of his grief:

> Mine eyes are full of tears, I cannot see;
> And yet salt water blinds them not so much
> But they can see a sort of traitors here.
>
> (IV. i. 244–6)

And in the lucidity of his perception he loses his identity: 'I have no name, no title' (IV. i. 255). Whereas the Queen could not name the future (Bolingbroke), Richard finds that the future, once arrived, destroys his self.

The perspective glass of tears in this scene is presented emblematically as a mirror – a solidified tear. Richard is not impressed with the reading of himself offered by this external eye. Bolingbroke observes (IV. i. 292–3) that by smashing the mirror Richard only uses superficial ritual ('the shadow of your sorrow') to destroy something unreal ('the shadow of your face'). Echoing the Queen's mental pregnancy metaphor Richard remarks,

> 'Tis very true, my grief lies all within;
> And these external manners of laments
> Are merely shadows to the unseen grief

That swells with silence in the tortur'd soul.
There lies the substance.

(IV. i. 294–8)

At this moment, faced with inescapable reality, Richard relaxes his grip on the symbolic world, learning that pageantry may accompany, but not be substituted for, real feeling. He acknowledges the flaws in a symbolic worldview, and comes to rely more fully on instinctive concepts.

In Richard's perceptual and conceptual birth through tears, as in Isabel's, the experience of grief involves cause of grief (internal; the substance) and method of lament (external; the shadow). Bushy minimises Isabel's cause ('More than your lord's departure weep not. More's not seen' – II. ii. 25), and she acknowledges some truth in his argument ('It may be so' – II. ii. 28). Bolingbroke criticises Richard's stylised grieving ('the shadow of your sorrow') and Richard admits the validity of his opinion (''tis very true'). Manner and form come together in tears when Richard and Isabel are parted, and their shared grief unites them in separation. Their tears, through which they perceive and create reality in moments of crisis, become factors which bind them together eternally. Their similar modes of apprehension and cognition, howsoever limited or imperfect, make their union in effect a marriage of true minds, symbolically compensating for their broken marriage. Richard asserts an indissoluble unity in paradoxes outrageous as any of Romeo's:

> two, together weeping, make one woe.

(v. i. 86)

> Come, come, in wooing sorrow let's be brief,
> Since, wedding it, there is such length in grief.

(v. i. 93–4)

Thus is 'woe to woe, sorrow to sorrow join'd'.

The concern with marriage and issue remains a strong theme for the rest of the play, through the Duke and Duchess of York's argument about the treachery of their son, Aumerle, and Bolingbroke's anxiety over young prince Hal ('Can no man tell me of my unthrifty son?' – v. iii. 1). In forcing Richard to a double

divorce (from spouse and country), Henry cements his own
marriage to the state. He finds himself inextricably bound to the
past, which nags him inwardly. Exton hears Henry's words, and
interprets the inexpressible plea of his glance:

> he wishtly look'd on me
> As who should say, 'I would thou wert the man
> That would divorce this terror from my heart';
> Meaning the king at Pomfret.

> (v. iv. 7–10)

The marital image leads straight to Pomfret (v. v), where Richard
enacts the third and last birth of the play, and the connection
between his cerebral 'marriage' and the York bickering scene (v. ii)
is apparent in Richard's use of the Duchess's lexical games and
quibbles in his meditation. This birth reflects on the past –
Bolingbroke's usurpation is now a *fait accompli*. Queen Isabel
foresaw it and Richard reacted to it in mental generative acts of a
similar nature, both conditioned by perception. Whereas Isabel
experienced labour pains, Richard detachedly analyses his conceit.
His act is more creative, to the extent that he *consciously* puts himself
through the thought-making process in order to broaden his
understanding of life:

> I have been studying how I may compare
> This prison where I live unto the world.

> (v. v. 1–2)

He is alone – 'here is not a creature but myself' (v. v. 4) – and
having difficulty in marshalling his ideas. We are not surprised at
this point to find Richard encouraging himself in matrimonial
metaphor. His experience has become part of the method he uses to
formulate thoughts:

> My brain I'll prove the female to my soul,
> My soul the father; and these two beget
> A generation of still-breeding thoughts,
> And these same thoughts people this little world,
> In humours like the people of this world.
> For no thought is contented.

> (v. v. 6–11)[35]

The thoughts which Richard creates and analyses reiterate the major themes of his life (as portrayed by the play): verbal values, ambition, content, the game of king and beggar, the nullity of death. Even the eye appears in equivocation: 'It is as hard to come as for a camel / To thread the postern of a small needle's eye' (v. v. 16–17).

Although the appeal of each thought is equivocally balanced with a grim glance at its implausibility, Richard's tone is far less cynical than in his homily on Death at Berkeley Castle (iii. ii. 152–70). At that point he had viewed flesh as a 'small model of the barren earth / Which serves as paste and cover to our bones' (iii. ii. 153–4) and ridiculed man's 'vain conceit' which persuades him of the impregnability of his body (iii. ii. 166–8). From these empty corporeal conceits Richard progresses at Pomfret to an earnest appraisal of the fruitful human soul. That he can grudgingly acknowledge the existence of love, despite his personal ruin, is a miracle.

Richard's halt at 'nothing' (v. v. 41) is really only the halfway house in his circular meditation. Eric La Guardia again gives an incomplete picture in ending his analysis here, for 'nothing, in a positive sense, did produce all things, and its formidableness in the genesis of man's affairs and dreams became for Shakespeare . . . a fertile obsession'.[36] Raised by music to a higher plane of thought, Richard soberly dissects his own governing symbols, in particular tears and breath, in relation to his misuse of time, and the result is the birth of a substantial thought. He finally recognises love as a real and valuable *something* ('a strange brooch'–v. v. 66) in this world, which was the original subject of his inquiry. He leaves the stage, still viewing life as a set of symbols, but having somehow learned to read the hieroglyphs in a more creative manner.

In *Richard II*, the generation metaphor can be compared to the *idée fixe* – a versatile motif, manifested through speech, symbol, and episode – which expresses the protagonists' groping toward knowledge. It reaches full maturity in Richard's deliberately initiated mental marriage and his positive conceptual analysis, but more or less dies with him. Bolingbroke ascends the throne as Henry IV, and moves on to the difficulties of actual parenthood in terms of a political and domestic struggle with Prince Hal.

In both *Richard II* and *Henry IV*, the passage of time is linked with creativity. In this connection, we may interestingly compare Richard's view of time, once he has attained self-awareness, with

Falstaff's hedonistic waste of it. Shakespeare employs the same itemisation of clock images in both cases:

RICHARD. I wasted time, and now doth Time waste me;
 For now hath Time made me his numb'ring clock.
 My thoughts are minutes; and with sighs they jar
 Their watches on unto mine eyes, the outward watch,
 Whereto my finger, like a dial's point,
 Is pointing still, in cleansing them from tears.

(v. v. 49–54)

Richard's tendency to melancholy introspection[37] dominates every minute of his time, in the same way that Falstaff's drinking, eating and wenching take up his. Compare Prince Hal's affectionate exchange with Falstaff at *1 Henry IV*, I. ii. 1, 6–13:

FALSTAFF. Now, Hal, what time of day is it, lad?
PRINCE. . . . What a devil hast thou to do with the time of the day? Unless hours were cups of sack, and minutes capons, and clocks the tongues of bawds, and dials the signs of leaping-houses, and the blessed sun himself a fair hot wench in flame-coloured taffeta, I see no reason why thou shouldest be so superfluous as to demand the time of the day.

At least Richard's mental marriage generates some productive thought; Falstaff reaches no such epiphany, as his own use of birth-imagery indicates: 'An I had but a belly of any indifferency, I were simply the most active fellow in Europe. My womb, my womb, my womb, undoes me' (*2 Henry IV*, IV. iii. 22–4). Since Falstaff is a type of 'bad father', bringing out the worst in Hal, Shakespeare does not accidentally use the obsolete *womb* ('stomach') to suggest his ruin. This grotesque parody of figurative pregnancy recurs in Falstaff's credo, which praises the creative virtue of alcohol and its enlivening effect on thought:

A good sherris-sack hath a two-fold operation in it. It ascends me into the brain; dries me there all the foolish and dull and crudy vapours which environ it; makes it apprehensive, quick, forgetive, full of nimble, fiery, and delectable shapes; which, delivered o'er to the voice, the tongue, which is the birth, becomes excellent wit. (*2 Henry IV*, IV. iii. 103–9)

The lamentably wasted time of *Richard II*, which at least sees a limited achievement in Richard's spiritual growth, is never redeemed in *Henry IV*.

Creativity resurfaces triumphantly in *Henry V* with the restoration of a legitimate royal line, succeeding by divine right. The perspective glass of tears, recording the misused time of *Richard II*, becomes the hourglass through which our fertile thoughts easily overleap multiple achievements. The mirror which reflected the corrupt Ricardian order is honourably reinstated in the person of Henry, 'the mirror of all Christian kings' (Prologue to Act II, l. 6). Whereas Richard underwent double divorce from spouse and country, Henry leads himself and England to marriage. All this fertility is aptly contained in the figure of the 'o', the womblike, cavernous theatre. Here, the creation of drama depends upon the audience's willingly imaginative construction (or 'amendment', as Theseus and Puck would say) of the dramatist's script:

> Think, when we talk of horses, that you see them . . .
> For 'tis your thoughts which now must deck our kings.

> (Prologue to Act I, ll. 26, 28)

The Chorus continually appeals to the audience's aural and optical sensitivity to help the play, for 'the task of shaping "airy nothing" is not peculiar to the poet. It is shared by all who imagine.'[38]

The relationship between aural perceptiveness and birth is a key theme of *Love's Labour's Lost*, sounded in Rosaline's stern reminder to Biron,

> A jest's prosperity lies in the ear
> Of him that hears it, never in the tongue
> Of him that makes it.

> (v. ii. 871–3)

Even at this early stage in Shakespeare's career, Rosaline's lesson is a hard one. Like *Richard II, Love's Labour's Lost* takes as part of its province the power of words and the importance of the listener's aural viewpoint, themes which underlie *Hamlet, Lear, Othello* and *Macbeth*.[39] The French female aristocrats completely misconstrue the serious protestations of Navarre, who could well complain, with Prufrock, 'That is not what I meant at all.'[40]

The play revolves around the idea of *wit*: 'wit' meaning knowledge, perspicuity, wisdom, and denoting especially that happy, fertile fancy which makes rhetorical conceits. The dialogue features a great many lines which contain peculiarly salty undertones. Herbert Ellis's glossary *Shakespeare's Lusty Punning in Love's Labour's Lost* recognises the prevalence of the dirty joke in this play. Perhaps Ellis's most important contribution is his entry at *wit*, for which he gives the following derivations:

> The familiar word *wit*, 'intelligence', 'understanding', etc., and the corresponding verb, are derived from OE *witan* 'to know', related to *witan* 'to see', also to G. *wissen* 'to know', L. *videre* 'to see'. . . . The other *wit* . . . was related to L. *vitalia* 'membra' and meant 'pudendum', masculine or feminine . . . the susceptibility of the two kinds of faculties to qualification by the same adjectives, such as those applying to size, vigor or debility, fertility or sterility, acuteness or bluntness, etc., provided not only ideal material for punsters but a convenient veil for naughty innuendoes as well.[41]

This definition has important thematic and linguistic ramifications for *Love's Labour's Lost.* That so much of the dialogue invites obscene interpretation is entirely compatible with the fact that the whole play, which after all explores the very nature of wit, teeters delicately on the boundary between carnal and cerebral knowledge.

Metaphors of sex and generation provide the natural vehicle for the play's major themes of mental and physical fruitfulness, and are particularly well suited to the badinage of the Navarre wits, the French female court, and the intellectual tensions and pretensions of Holofernes, Nathaniel and Dull. The fertile fancy reveals itself in the birth of eloquence, and characters perceive rhetorical and intellectual achievement in the context of mental generation. But in using these metaphors they implicitly acknowledge the human sexual urge and procreative impulse, which share the same linguistic expressions. And herein lies the comedy, encapsulated beautifully by Costard's pertinent comment after a particularly 'greasy' set of *double entendres*:

> O' my troth, most sweet jests! most incony vulgar wit!
> When it comes so smoothly off, so obscenely, as it were, so fit.

(IV. i. 144–5)

The word 'incony', punning ingeniously on 'in-cunny', fitly characterises the play's verbal humour. None of the characters is above a dirty joke; none of them can escape dirty jokes, given the idiom in which they define themselves and view their world.

Almost all the characters strive toward creativity. Biron reacts instinctively against the ascetic pursuit of knowledge proposed by the King of Navarre, to whose programme of 'barren tasks' (I. i. 47) he has pledged himself. Unlike the King, who compares him to a killer frost biting the 'first-born infants of the spring' (I. i. 101), Biron fears the misplacement of his creative energy: 'Why should I joy in any abortive birth?' (I. i. 104). The French women rate the men in terms of their creative wit, singling it out as their most remarkable characteristic. The Princess sets the equivocal tone in her courtly rebuke of Boyet:

> I am less proud to hear you tell my worth
> Than you much willing to be counted wise
> In spending your wit in the praise of mine.

> (II. i. 17–19)

To all the girls except Rosaline, excessive wit is a negative trait. Only Rosaline appreciates wit as a pregnant, lively quality, and she praises Biron in an extended generation metaphor:

> His eyes begets occasion for his wit,
> For every object that the one doth catch
> The other turns to a mirth-moving jest,
> Which his fair tongue, conceit's expositor,
> Delivers in such apt and gracious words
> That aged ears play truant at his tales,
> And younger hearings are quite ravished;
> So sweet and voluble is his discourse.

> (II. i. 69–76)

These values are sharply satirised in Act IV scene ii, where Holofernes, Nathaniel and Dull conduct a learned disquisition upon the hunt. Nathaniel favourably contrasts the fertile brains of himself and Holofernes with the stunted mentality of Dull:

> Sir, he hath never fed of the dainties that are bred in a book;

> He hath not eat paper, as it were; he hath not drunk ink; his
> intellect is not replenished; he is only an animal, only sensible in
> the duller parts;
> And such barren plants are set before us, that we thankful should
>   be,
> Which we of taste and feeling are, for those parts that do fructify
>   in us more than he.

> (IV. ii. 25–30)

This dubious fruitfulness manifests itself in Holofernes's verbal gift.
He offers an astonishing analysis of the hunt, in a piece of doggerel
which contrives to be stultifyingly obscure and shamelessly lewd at
the same time:

> The preyful princess pierc'd and prick'd a pretty pleasing pricket;
> Some say a sore; but not a sore, till now made sore with shooting.
> The dogs did yell; put 'ell to sore, then sorel jumps from thicket;
> Or pricket sore, or else sore'll the people fall a-hooting.
> If sore be sore, then 'ell to sore makes fifty sores – O – sorel!
> Of one sore I an hundred make, by adding but one more l.

> (IV. ii. 55–60)

There is nothing moral in this at all. In his utter failure to 'abrogate
scurrility' (IV. ii. 56), Holofernes accidentally and unwittingly
cracks the symbolic code of the hunt scene (IV. i). The men's
spiritual hunt for fame (I. i), a barren endeavour, yields to the juicy
animal hunt conducted by the women, where the horned deer is
shot. And now Holofernes expatiates self-satisfiedly on his rhetorical
fertility:

> This is a gift that I have, simple, simple; a foolish extravagant
> spirit, full of forms, figures, shapes, objects, ideas, apprehensions,
> motions, revolutions. These are begot in the ventricle of memory,
> nourish'd in the womb of *pia mater*, and delivered upon the
> mellowing of occasion. But the gift is good in those in whom it is
> acute, and I am thankful for it.   (IV. ii. 64–70)

The jargon of the Renaissance medical text provides the semantic
springboard for Holofernes's elaborate pun.[42] With superbly unconscious irony, he uses the metaphor of the lower quarters to

illustrate his refined consciousness. Using similar idiom, Nathaniel and Holofernes close out the episode by unconsciously revealing how 'sensible in the duller parts' they themselves are:

> NATHANIEL. Sir, I praise the Lord for you, and so may my parishioners; for . . . their daughters profit very greatly under you. . .
>
> HOLOFERNES. *Mehercle* . . . if their daughters be capable, I will put it to them.
>
> (IV. ii. 75–82)[43]

The wit of Nathaniel and Holofernes, rooted in sexuality, may be compared to that of the Navarre wits, which the girls disdain as 'folly, in wisdom hatch'd' (v. ii. 71). What at a distance appeared creative to the women seems self-centred and unfunny close up. They temporarily lose their taste for the Navarre wits, mocking their conventionalised attempts at courtship (the glove, the necklace, the mile-long letter). With great relish, the girls chastise the men for their unproductive wit and wreck their carefully planned Muscovite project. But this destructiveness is symptomatic of a deeper delight which the Princess experiences in watching enterprises abort:

> That sport best pleases which doth least know how;
> Where zeal strives to content, and the contents
> Dies in the zeal of that which it presents.
> Their form confounded makes most form in mirth,
> When great things labouring perish in their birth.
>
> (v. ii. 517–21)

She refers to the disastrous entertainment of the commoners, but Biron does not miss her oblique hint at Navarre's unfruitful wooing: 'A right description of our sport, my lord' (v. ii. 522).

With heightened self-awareness, Biron describes the infantile impressionability of love:

> love is full of unbefitting strains,
> All wanton as a child, skipping, and vain,
> Form'd by the eye and therefore, like the eye,
> Full of strange shapes, of habits, and of forms,

> Varying in subjects as the eye doth roll
> To every varied object in his glance.
>
> (v. ii. 770–5)

The very theory of Theseus! But this is no dream, for Mercade's entrance brings Death into the green world of the play. The Princess's cruel remark turns out to be a right description of everybody's sport. And Biron's summation, 'Our wooing doth not end like an old play;/Jack hath not Jill' (v. ii. 884–5), contrasts grimly with Puck's: 'Jack shall have Jill; / Nought shall go ill; / The man will have his mare again, and all shall be well' (*A Midsummer Night's Dream*, III. ii. 461–3). Rosaline imposes a penance on Biron with the specific aim of mitigating his excessive creativity: 'To weed this wormwood from your fruitful brain' (v. ii. 857). Using the metaphor of generation to the end, she forces Biron to the realisation that his

> influence is begot of that loose grace
> Which shallow laughing hearers give to fools.
>
> (v. ii. 869–70)

His exile in a hospital, conversing with the sick, will teach him the true source of a joke's *prosperity*. And 'prosperity' here means 'growth' as well as 'success'.[44]

So *Love's Labour's Lost*. Or is it? Ironically enough, the real baby in the play is borne by the illiterate Jacquenetta, though in fairly verbal terms: it 'brags in her belly already' (v. ii. 683). Jacquenetta cannot read; she delivers letters to the wrong people; she is probably incapable of rhetorical conceit; but, in one of Shakespeare's finest ironies, she does conceive. Armado's three-year vow to 'hold the plough' for Jacquenetta's love (v. ii. 892–3) parallels the King's three-year programme of asceticism, with which the play started. The metaphor of generation in *Love's Labour's Lost* defines creative endeavour, an endeavour which proclaims itself in conceit, the issue of the 'quick', 'hot' and 'apt' wit the characters display. Shakespeare's final image-inversion is devastating: Holofernes's brain, full of verbiage, is like an expectant mother. Jacquenetta, an expectant mother, carries in her womb a baby who 'brags'.

Shakespeare's lyrical plays share a basic 'conceptual' quality in that his characters are above all concerned with realising their fullest potential through the generation of fruitful thought or action. This concern never fades. The metaphor of generation continues as its prime expression. Taking the language of pregnancy which his contemporaries applied to their own poetic methods, Shakespeare refashioned it for the drama and made it an integral element of his characters' existence. The parallels he draws between the workings of womb and brain subtly modify the reader's understanding of his bawdy humour. To see only a 'puden-synomy' suggested by various types of o figure[45] is reductive of Shakespeare's invention, for within the zero lies the potential for creation. Hence its lasting popularity as womb-symbol, and hence also the dramatic tension, so powerful in Shakespeare, between *something* and *nothing*. There is also a 'womb-synomy' here, represented by o figures such as the eye, the theatre, the brain – all loci of creation, and all terms of reference introduced in the lyrical plays. We should regard the Shakespearian o with great caution, not dismissing it as merely a bawdy figure representing the female pudendum or syphilitic spots. The big, womby o, in all its forms, may refer to the theatre (the Globe) to 'the great globe itself' (*The Tempest*, IV. i. 153) and the countries within it which give birth to the drama being chronicled, to the generative mind of a character, the interpretative mind of the audience, the fluid and fecund brain of the dramatist.

The lyrical plays establish these images and symbols, which form the basis of Shakespeare's generation metaphor. It is with these correspondences and associations in mind that his succeeding dramas may be viewed. The later comedies explore animal (*As You Like It*) and spiritual (*The Merchant of Venice*) forces which attract masculine and feminine, and the themes of real and figurative pregnancy are amplified in the problem plays, where the expectancy of actual children comes increasingly to dominate the dramatic action. Shakespeare turns to the problem of sexual intercourse, enmeshing with actual pregnancy the pregnant wit which fires the lyrical plays. That, of course, proves a problem indeed.

3 ' 'Tis Very Pregnant': The Problem Plays

E. M. W. Tillyard, at a loss for a critical term to cover the dramaturgical phenomenon that concerned him, made a prescient suggestion in the introduction to *Shakespeare's Problem Plays*: 'to achieve the necessary elasticity and inclusiveness, consider the connotations of the parallel term "problem child" '.[1] The term is supremely appropriate, although not for the same reasons which Tillyard had in mind when he picked it. Tillyard chose to emphasise the *problem* element. According to his analysis, the plays either display problems (*Hamlet, Troilus and Cressida*), or, quite simply, are problems (*All's Well That Ends Well, Measure for Measure*). Critics had a field day with the 'problem play' question, the issue boiling down to the dual nature of the plays. Their tragic set-up with comic resolution perplexed many scholars. Frustratingly, the plays elude generic classification: 'it is the mood of the tragedies, without the ultimate tragic end', wrote W. W. Lawrence,[2] who preferred to call the plays 'Problem Comedies', ignored *Hamlet*, and explored *Cymbeline* instead.

Certainly, then, a problem. But why is *child* appropriate? It is an important element in this group of plays. The plots of Shakespeare's early plays, in particular the comedies, hinge on courtship and marriage; the plots of his tragedies are concerned with children and family relationships. In the middle are the problem plays, which deal with sexual encounter and pregnancy. The problem plays represent a quite natural stage in Shakespeare's shift of interest from lovers to families.

Shakespeare's development of the theme of mistaken identity clearly anticipates his confrontation in the problem plays with sex and birth. In the early plays, with the exception of *The Two Gentlemen of Verona*, the dramatist controls optical error. When the characters attempt to initiate error, as in the Muscovite episode in *Love's Labour's Lost* (v. i) or Tamora's persuasion scene in *Titus*

Andronicus (IV. ii), they fail miserably. But with Oberon's herb-squeezing in *A Midsummer Night's Dream* comes a radical change. Henceforward, Shakespeare allows his protagonists the ability to reshape themselves in disguise. In the succeeding comedies (*Much Ado About Nothing, The Merchant of Venice, As You Like It, Twelfth Night*), disguise is usually undertaken by a woman in the context of premarital courtship. As Shakespeare's career progresses, disguise deepens into substitution. A notable advance in plot takes place between his last two 'romantic' comedies. In *As You Like It*, Rosalind/Ganymede sets up Silvius as an alternative partner for Phebe with Phebe's full knowledge and permission (they all confirm this arrangement in V. ii). A marriage between Rosalind and Phebe would be biologically impossible, although never likely anyway, since denouement prevents it. But in *Twelfth Night* the situation is more complex. The possibility of an all-female marriage demands the substitution of a spouse. Faced with the all-to-be-avoided union of Olivia and Viola/Cesario, Shakespeare has Olivia marry Sebastian (Viola's convenient twin) before the denouement, believing that he is Cesario. All these confusions are harmless and comical because we are still in the world of the cardboard-figure *commedia dell'arte* marriages of the comedies. Sexual intercourse never enters the question. With *Twelfth Night* and the substituted spouse, Shakespeare reached the limits of transsexual disguise as a dramatic device. The comedies, although romantic, are not erotic, and rarely does the reality of sex cloud their automatic and inevitable springtime unions. The implicit sex-urge surfaces slowly in the problem plays, as Shakespeare's plots move from spouse-substitution to bedmate-substitution, with a resultant loss of innocence that prepares us for tragedy.

These developments in plot are paralleled by Shakespeare's increasingly assured dramatic use of the metaphor of generation. We have already noted the tendency in his early plays to define thought as a living entity whose character is dictated by the perceptions and perspectives of the fertile mind. This lively image was used in rarefied and intellectual play, whether with comic or tragic overtones, to describe the formation of ideas. It was particularly well suited to the 'shape-making', especially optical, in which the early characters indulge, and constituted a key element in the development of the 'something-out-of-nothing' theme. In Shakespeare's dialogue, the sexual impulse manifested itself through bouts of bawdy, sallies of wit, flights of fecund poetic imagination, fruitful dream. Generation metaphor distinguished and defined all these activities, which contribute to the mental experience of his early characters. Towards the middle of Shakespeare's career, the mental horizons of his protagonists widen considerably. Fanciful cerebral endeavours broaden into sophisticated cognitive processes, accompanied by a more mature use of generation metaphor, adapting itself to accommodate deeper significance. With the problem plays, the ludic *conceit* becomes the altogether weightier *conception*, a word that makes its first appearance in *Twelfth Night*, the dark comedy which rounds off Shakespeare's 'summer' period, and which precedes *Hamlet* by about one year.

Another word whose overtones become more complex is *pregnant*. In the early Renaissance, 'pregnant' generally meant 'full of meaning', but the sense 'with child' was certainly inferrable from Latin and Italian cognates.[3] The *OED* quotes the earliest occurrence of 'pregnant' meaning 'with child' at around 1545. Contemporary with Shakespeare's early writings, John Donne emphasises this sense in his opening lines to 'The Extasie':

> Where, like a pillow on a bed,
> A pregnant bank swell'd up, to rest
> The violet's reclining head,
> Sat we two, one another's best.[4]

The Renaissance pregnant poetic lent added topical and cultural weight to the development of both senses of the word. In 1604, Robert Cawdrey's *A Table Alphabeticall* makes the double meaning of 'pregnant' official: he glosses the word as signifying 'wittie, substantiall, with child'.[5] In the problem plays, Shakespeare's development of generation metaphor includes some innovative improvisation on 'pregnant' and its contrary, which he coined: 'unpregnant'.

Generation fulfils a double function in the problem plays of Shakespeare. On the one hand, it appears in metaphor; on the other, it gradually comes to occupy pivotal plot and structural importance as well. The language of generation constitutes an important metaphor in *Hamlet* and *Troilus and Cressida*; the act of generation is a prime mover of the plot of *All's Well That Ends Well*. At the pinnacle of Shakespeare's achievement in this period,

Measure for Measure effects the synthesis of language and act, eloquently expressing the inevitable human procreative impulse by a full integration of the theme, plot, and language of generation. This chapter will survey *Hamlet, Troilus and Cressida* and *All's Well* before passing on to a detailed look at *Measure for Measure*.

In *Hamlet*, Shakespeare uses the generation metaphor sparingly, though effectively, to underscore the theme of fruitful action. The thinker's brain teems with embryonic resolution, which awaits timely delivery. And, although Hamlet berates himself for his indecorous delay, and his inability to put theory into practice, other characters do not share his low esteem of his creative power. When Hamlet deliberately misconstrues Polonius's invitation to walk 'out of the air' (i.e. 'indoors') as 'Into my grave?' (ii. ii. 208–10) Polonius observes, 'How *pregnant* sometimes his replies are! a happiness that often madness hits on, which reason and sanity could not so *prosperously* be *deliver'd* of' (ii. ii. 212–14, emphasis added). Polonius's aside occurs after Hamlet warns him against letting Ophelia walk in the sun, for fear she may conceive. Hamlet would dispatch Ophelia to a nunnery, where no babies can be made (iii. i. 122–3), but in his talk with Polonius he draws a careful, punning distinction between 'conception' = 'pregnancy' and 'conception' = 'understanding': 'Let her not walk i' th' sun. Conception is a blessing, but not as your daughter may conceive' (ii. ii. 185–7). Hamlet here refers to the popular belief that the sun created a warm enough environment for spontaneous generation, and extends the superstition to cover human generation.[6] He himself is moved to cerebral conception. At his first appearance in the play, Hamlet cites being 'too much i' th' sun' (i. ii. 67) to Claudius as the reason for his moody melancholy. Here, of course, there is a homophonic pun on *sun/son*,[7] and the line is often interpreted as Hamlet's bitter reflection on his subordinate rank. If we apply the *sun/son* pun to Hamlet's warning about Ophelia, his lines acquire the following secondary meaning: 'Don't let Ophelia anywhere near me, the king's son. Understanding is a blessing, but I might make her pregnant.' Given the fertilising power of the sun, Hamlet's implication to Claudius appears to be: 'my enforced filial relationship to you impregnates me mentally'. This reading is supported by Claudius's echo of Polonius's pregnant language in describing Hamlet's mental state:

> There's something in his soul
> O'er which his melancholy sits on brood,

> And I do doubt the hatch and the disclose
> Will be some danger.[8]
>
> (iii. i. 172–5)

In contrast to Claudius and Polonius, Hamlet feels himself to be tragically inert and unproductive, to the extent that he cannot follow the course of action which his situation demands by redressing the offence which has been perpetrated. He contrasts himself with flattering courtiers, who, scenting profit, 'crook the pregnant hinges of the knee' (iii. ii. 66).[9] Hamlet's relationship with the Players, and the play – *The Mousetrap* – which he rescripts for them make plain the importance to him of motivated thought creatively transferred into action. These ideas are cryptically conveyed – one might almost say, 'hidden' – in the First Player's Pyrrhus speech, given upon arrival at the castle, and in his caution, as Player King, to a too-much-protesting Player Queen. Let us consider these utterances individually. At Hamlet's request, the First Player continues the Pyrrhus speech which he started. He describes Pyrrhus, on the point of furiously killing Priam, neutralised by a momentary pause:

> as a painted tyrant, Pyrrhus stood
> And, like a neutral to his will and matter,
> Did nothing.
>
> (ii. ii. 502–4)

Hamlet is in exactly the same position as Pyrrhus, unable to effect a fertile marriage of his will and matter (i.e. his *cause*, of which we shall hear more from Othello). He is miserably aware of his lack of pregnant readiness. Envying the creative ability of the Player to suit 'forms to his conceit' and sensible of his own barren procrastination, he soliloquises,

> I,
> A dull and muddy-mettled rascal, peak
> Like John-a-dreams, unpregnant of my cause,
> And can say nothing.
>
> (ii. ii. 593–6)

The similarity between neutral Pyrrhus, doing nothing, and unpregnant Hamlet, saying nothing, is striking – and intentional. Once again, Shakespeare has concealed the central idea of the play in the very centre of the play.

Hamlet's view of himself as unpregnant is strangely at odds with the views of Polonius and Claudius. Why the inconsistency? Again, we look to his relationship with the Players. His instructions to the troupe reveal that he favours a calm approach to passion: 'in the very torrent, tempest, and, as I may say, the whirlwind of passion, you must acquire and beget a temperance that may give it smoothness' (III. ii. 6–9). This stipulation may be fine as far as art is concerned, but it does not produce satisfactory results in real life. Temperance, begot of reflection, is potentially disastrous in terms of actually getting anything done, as Hamlet had observed in the previous scene:

> the native hue of resolution
> Is sicklied o'er with the pale cast of thought,
> And enterprises of great pith and moment
> With this regard their currents turn awry,
> And lose the name of action.

> (III. i. 84–8)

Reflection kills the pith, the nucleus, the life of enterprise. The Player King gives the watchword for the whole play when he describes the enfeebling effect of delay upon human resolve:

> I do believe you think what now you speak,
> But what we do determine oft we break.
> Purpose is but the slave to memory,
> Of violent birth, but poor validity.

> (III. ii. 196–9)

In *Macbeth*, we will find the hero vowing to himself: 'This deed I'll do now ere this purpose cool' (IV. ii. 154). And Macbeth, who does what cannot be undone, is beset by the thoughts which succeed, rather than precede, a deed. Shakespeare's tragedies run the gamut of man's attitudes to action: from reserve (*Hamlet*) to remorse (*Macbeth*), from 'I can't bring myself to do it' to 'Oh God, I've done it now.' Hamlet has no trouble birthing his purpose, but his long delay argues its 'poor validity'. We shall see later how Macbeth deals with the child-as-future which his precipitate action delivers.

Hamlet's preoccupation with death and evil,[10] which places it with the other tragedies, should not blind us to its images of life. While I would not go so far as to suggest that *Hamlet* explores the theme of birth, I would contend that its darkly equivocal language prepares us for the pregnant world of *Measure for Measure*. The generation metaphor serves as both rhetorical illustration and dramatic comment, manifesting a technical advance quite in line with Shakespeare's development from decorative to organic imagery. Those who seek the 'regeneration' of Hamlet[11] should remember that he always affirms life, and that his refusal to step into his grave is a 'pregnant' reply. Wolfgang Clemen makes a pertinent remark, centring his sights on Hamlet with an emphatic – and, probably, unconscious – generation metaphor. It seems that Claudius and Polonius are not alone in recognising Hamlet's innate fertility and the boundless potential of his brain, even if Hamlet himself would not agree: 'It is Hamlet who creates the most significant images, images marking the atmosphere and theme of the play, which are paler and less pregnant in the speech of the other characters.'[12]

Written shortly after *Hamlet*, or concurrently with it, *Troilus and Cressida* also employs generation metaphor as rhetorical figure, and, in a sense, also as an extra choric voice, commenting with profound irony on both the Trojan war, fought over an illicit affair, and the barren liaison of Troilus and Cressida. Caroline Spurgeon has rightly remarked Shakespeare's full development in this play of one of his favourite images:

> Time as a nurse, breeder, and begetter . . . bringing to birth and maturing seeds or germs . . . the medium, the necessary condition by the aid of which events, qualities, projects, ideas, and thoughts are born into actual and material being.[13]

Ulysses's remark to Nestor 'I have a young conception in my brain; / Be you my time to bring it to some shape' (I. iii. 312–13) is just one of a multitude of birth-images in Act I scene iii, where the Greeks review the success of their Trojan campaign. Agamemnon sets the tone for the scene in his opening lines, rich in *double entendre*:

The ample proposition that hope makes
In all designs begun on earth below
Fails in the promis'd largeness.

(i. iii. 3–5)

In words which amplify Theseus's image in *A Midsummer Night's Dream*, v. i. 17, Agamemnon describes how the Greeks' action has failed to measure up to 'that unbodied figure of the thought / That gave't surmised shape' (i. iii. 16–17). The entire discussion between Ulysses and Nestor regarding Hector's challenge and the respective merits of Achilles and Ajax echoes Agamemnon's imagery of birth. The emerging political scene is presented as a newborn baby when Nestor remarks that the fight will be useful in predicting the outcome of the whole war; it

shall give a scantling
Of good or bad unto the general;
And in such indexes, although small pricks
To their subsequent volumes, there is seen
The baby figure of the giant mass
Of things to come at large.

(i. iii. 341–6)

Perhaps if Shakespeare had limited his generation metaphor to developing the political context of the play, we should not have found him overly adventurous. His real master-stroke consists in the employment of the generation metaphor for the inner plot, which deals with the abortive affair of Troilus and Cressida. We may see the effectiveness of this double use in an interesting parallel between the utterances of Ulysses in Act III scene iii and Cressida in Act I scene ii. Of caution Ulysses states,

The providence that's in a watchful state
Knows almost every grain of Plutus' gold,
Finds bottom in th' uncomprehensive deeps,
Keeps place with thought and almost, like the gods,
Does thoughts unveil in their dumb cradles.

(III. iii. 196–200)

The watchfulness which produces newborn ideas . . . Cressida's

idea of 'a watchful state' is very different from Ulysses's, and results
in a different kind of birth. At her first appearance, she bawdily
describes to Pandarus one of her 'thousand watches': 'If I cannot
ward what I would not have hit, I can watch you for telling how I
took the blow; unless it swell past hiding, and then it's past
watching' (I. ii. 292–5). Cressida jokes about actual pregnancy,
and, despite her assumed coolness, reveals her lust for Troilus easily
enough. Using the metaphor of maternity, she confesses the
inefficiency of her watch, and her failure to dissemble: 'My thoughts
were like unbridled children, grown / Too headstrong for their
mother' (III. ii. 130–1).

The pregnant promise of emotional fulfilment is not realised in
the union of Troilus and Cressida, which is doomed to miscarry. In
an image of abortion, Troilus laments their sudden parting, forced
upon them by political expediency:

> injury of chance
> Puts back leave-taking, justles roughly by
> All time of pause, rudely beguiles our lips
> Of all rejoindure, forcibly prevents
> Our lock'd embrasures, strangles our dear vows
> Even in the birth of our own labouring breath.

> (IV. iv. 35–40)

Such abortiveness, and especially expressed in this imagery, invites
comparison with *Love's Labour's Lost*.[14] In both plays, the sense of
pregnant effort leading to abortive conclusion runs very strongly.
Troilus deplores the consignment of Cressida to the sexy and
seductive Greeks, measuring his own inferiority in these words:

> I cannot sing,
> Nor heel the high lavolt, nor sweeten talk,
> Nor play at subtle games – fair virtues all,
> To which the Grecians are most prompt and pregnant.

> (IV. iv. 87–90)

The image of pregnancy appropriately expresses the relationship
between Troilus and Cressida, where, as Hamlet observed of
Claudius and Gertrude, 'reason panders will' (*Hamlet*, III. iv. 88). In
this play we even have a character called Pandarus, whose lustful

lifestyle is etched in a generation metaphor from the lusty Paris: 'He eats nothing but doves . . . and that breeds hot blood, and hot blood begets hot thoughts, and hot thoughts beget hot deeds, and hot deeds is love' (III. i. 140–3). 'Is this', an indignant and pained Pandarus responds, 'the generation of love?' (III. i. 144). The barren Trojan war parallels the abortive course of love in *Troilus and Cressida*; the metaphor of generation is ironically used to portray both events.

Shakespeare often handled similar themes with contrasted perspectives in consecutive plays. As we saw in Chapter 2, *A Midsummer Night's Dream* inverts the dramatic priorites of *Romeo and Juliet*. The treatments of leadership and loyalty are diametrically opposed in *Henry V* and *Julius Caesar*. In the same way, the generative quality of *All's Well*[15] contrasts with the political and sexual sterility of *Troilus and Cressida*. Whereas *Troilus* closes with abortive separation after unproductive, illicit sex, and an unconcluded Trojan war, *All's Well* ends with a legitimate pregnancy and a political peace.

Shakespeare's ironic recall of *Troilus and Cressida* is openly apparent in *All's Well That Ends Well*. He significantly changes his heroine's name from the source's 'Giletta' to Helena. The Clown urges the Trojan association in his doggerel when sent to bring her to the Countess:

> Was this fair face the cause, quoth she,
>   Why the Grecians sacked Troy?
> Fond done, done fond . . .
>   Was this King Priam's joy?

> (I. iii. 74–8)

The courtier Lafew equates Helena with Cressida when leaving her to cure the King, comparing his role in their meeting, which leads to a fertile marriage, to Pandarus's sexual procurement: 'I am Cressid's uncle, / That dare leave two together' (II. i. 90–1). Unlike her mythical namesakes, however, this Helen, this Cressid, turns out to be a fecund, redemptive source. Shakespeare reverses the infertile assumptions of *Troilus and Cressida*, using deliberate verbal and thematic echoes to make the contrast plain.

In *All's Well*, a chief virtue of sexual intercourse resides in its procreative power. As in *Troilus*, love and war are interlinked, this time with fertile overtones, since the most outspoken praise of procreative sex comes from a soldier, Parolles. Although, as a true follower of Mars, Parolles extols sex without mentioning marriage,[16] those arguments which stress generation rather than the pleasure principle inspire his most memorable axioms against virginity: 'Loss of virginity is rational increase. . . . To speak on the part of virginity is to accuse your mothers. . . . Virginity murders itself . . .' (i. i. 137–8, 148–9, 151).

Helena emphasises the generative function of sex within marriage when requesting the freedom to choose her mate, desiring 'My low and humble name to *propagate* / With any branch or image of thy state' (ii. i. 200–1, emphasis added).

A most interesting contrastive echo with *Troilus and Cressida*, and the play's most eloquent plea for procreation, occurs in the Clown Lavatch's request to be released from service in order to marry: 'Service is no heritage; and I think I shall never have the blessing of God till I have issue o' my body; for they say barnes are blessings' (i. iii. 25–8). The word 'service' is double-edged, referring both to domestic servitude and sexual service, and the Clown's speech thus acquires a significant second meaning: 'There is no future in sexual dalliance; I must marry and found a family.' The sexual pun on 'service'[17] points up the relationship with *Troilus and Cressida*: illicit sexual encounter is sterile, offering no promise of children. Only marriage assures survival – 'heritage', 'blessing of God' – through procreation.

How simple it would be if the Clown's rationale ended here. But he has other reasons for contemplating matrimony: 'My poor body, madam, requires it' (i. iii. 30). The conflicting aims of libido and soul, juxtaposed in Lavatch's plea, illustrate the all-too-human sexual double standard. Sex is honourably procreative, but also sinful, necessary fun.[18] It provides the only means of 'eternity', while also helping to make the present more enjoyable. The Clown's paradoxical view embodies concern for the hereafter as well as the here-and-now, adding an extra dimension to the pursuit of generative, virtuous monogamy in *All's Well That Ends Well*, and shadowing forth the sexual casuistry of *Measure for Measure*.

All's Well That Ends Well is a transitional piece, whose generative theme, while negating the sterility of *Troilus and Cressida*, also sounds the more complex themes of *Measure for Measure* in several anticipatory notes. The admonitory Mariana of *All's Well*, wise to masculine perfidy, has a contrasted namesake in *Measure for Measure*'s sexually duped Mariana. The verbally uninhibited

Parolles, slandering his lord to his face (albeit unwittingly), develops into the foul-mouthed, calumniating Lucio of *Measure for Measure*. Remarkably, Shakespeare chooses to name his next heroine, Isabella, after the Clown's unseen girlfriend, Isbel. Both girls cause the sexual double standard to come into operation, and both are linked through a bifurcated perception of sex as saintly and sinful. The coincidence of name and motif from *Troilus and Cressida* toward *Measure for Measure* indicates a conscious development by Shakespeare of the procreative theme.

Measure for Measure brings to perfection the new techniques of plot and language which Shakespeare had developed in *Hamlet*, *Troilus and Cressida* and *All's Well That Ends Well*. In it the action and imagery of generation coalesce. The metaphor of generation is both container and contents, since the plot, which deals with pregnancy, is unravelled in the most appropriate language – the metaphor of pregnancy. At this stage in Shakespeare's career, then, the metaphor functions as 'concept presented and as a form of presentation'.[19] A quick illustration will suffice at this point. On the literal level, Mrs Elbow is pregnant; on the metaphorical level, Angelo, analysing motive, says,

> 'tis very pregnant,
> The jewel that we find, we stoop and take't,
> Because we see it.

> (II. i. 23–5)

Action and image are one, and the tension between real and metaphorical pregnancy propels the drama forward.

A growing recognition of the importance of pregnancy in the play has pushed modern criticism of *Measure for Measure* onto grounds unchartered by earlier critics, who saw the play in terms of its ethical framework only.[20] Undoubtedly, our franker attitudes towards sex permit broader views of the play. Where pre-1970 criticism dwelt upon the play's sources, its Christian themes, its historical importance (as flattery of James I, for example), modern readings respond more sensitively to its physical side, or, more accurately, to its concern with man's physical instincts. The design of *Measure for Measure* actually invites this kind of inner probing. It is the perfect play for prurient minds. Angelo's frigid rectitude masks his lust, which reveals itself in his language. In the same way, the entire play's concern with justice, grace and so forth is but a polite veneer which hides the underlying sexual theme. But, here again, a careful reading shows how constantly Shakespeare keeps before us the play's underside, in action, character development and metaphor.

The play's iterative images of increase (including fruit and essence images), form and impression, weight, and carriage and motion are all component parts of the conception metaphor. Increase stands for the human creative potential; form, impression, coining refer to the 'stamping' of a new identity upon a new. individual; and weight, carriage and motion complete the experience of the pregnant woman. It is therefore particularly appropriate that the character of Juliet[21] should unite these four major image-clusters, since her pregnant state is the dramatic *a priori* from which the entire plot proceeds. Claudio first mentions her, using the coining and stamping imagery of Act I scene i:

> The stealth of our most mutual entertainment
> With character too gross is writ on Juliet.
>
> (I. ii. 143–4)

Lucio tells Isabel Claudio's news in the grossest images of increase:

> Your brother and his lover have embrac'd;
> As those that feed grow full, as blossoming time
> That from the seedness the bare fallow brings
> To teeming foison, even so her plenteous womb
> Expresseth his full tilth and husbandry.
>
> (I. iv. 40–4)

Informing Isabel of Claudio's predicament is Lucio's 'pith of business' (I. iv. 70). Interrogating Juliet, the disguised Duke puns on the idea of carriage:

> DUKE. Repent you, fair one, of the sin you carry?
> JULIET. I do; and bear the same most patiently.
>
> (II. iii. 19–20)

We recall the 'women of good carriage' in Mercutio's account of the fertilising visit of Queen Mab (*Romeo and Juliet*, I. iv. 94). The Duke condemns Juliet's share in the sin, using the play's iterative weight image:

DUKE. So then it seems your most offenceful act
   Was mutually committed?
JULIET.   Mutually.
DUKE. Then was your sin of heavier kind than his.

(II. iii. 26–8)

It is finely ironic that no one can say exactly what was done to
Mrs Elbow, despite the free use of pregnancy imagery in *Measure for
Measure*. Kate Keep-down was impregnated by Lucio. By the end of
the play, we may safely assume, Mariana is pregnant, and Isabella
may shortly become pregnant. Thus the context of the dramatic
action is defined. Masculine characters, localities, events, are also
portrayed in generation imagery, either by way of the four image-
clusters just described, or through simple wordplay and pun, which
render the message uncompromisingly clear. For example, invest-
ing Escalus with civic responsibility, the Duke says,

> The nature of our people,
> Our city's institutions, and the terms
> For common justice, y'are as pregnant in
> As art and practice hath enriched any
> That we remember.

(I. I. 9–13)

Perhaps suggestive of 'ideal paternity'[22] are those images of
impression and coining which Duke Vincentio applies to Angelo's
governmental abilities: 'bid come before us Angelo. / What figure of
us, think you, he will bear?' (I. i. 15–16). The Duke's hasty departure
from Vienna is of 'quick condition' (I. i. 53). He seems to have a
premonition of birth, and he is quite right.

Angelo, left to govern the city and quell the fever of fornication in
its suburbs, presents his own view in pregnancy imagery. This
feature of his language gives the lie to his unctuously virtuous
bearing. Vienna itself becomes a foetus-bearing womb in his
description of the reawakening law:

> The law hath not been dead, though it hath slept . . .
>
>   Now 'tis awake,
> Takes note of what is done, and like a prophet
> Looks in a glass that shows what future evils,

> Either new, or by remissness new conceiv'd,
> And so in progress to be hatch'd and born,
> Are now to have no successive degrees,
> But ere they live, to end.

(II. ii. 91, 94–100)

He intends no mercy to the young fornicator Claudio, who has got Juliet pregnant. But Isabella's supplication plants new ideas in his mind, impregnating him mentally with an as-yet-unconscious desire to corrupt her: 'She speaks, and 'tis such sense / That my sense breeds with it' (II. ii. 142–3). By the time Angelo and Isabel meet again, in Act II scene iv, he has decided on a bargain: her virginity saves her brother's head. He loses touch with his spiritual nature, expressing his alienation thus:

> Heaven in my mouth,
> As if I did but only chew his name,
> And in my heart the strong and swelling evil
> Of my conception.

(II. iv. 4–7)

The structural placing of the dialogue between Juliet and the Friar/Duke (II. iii) is immensely important. It occurs between Act II scene ii, where Angelo is first attracted to Isabel, and Act II scene iv, where he decides to blackmail her sexually, and propositions her. Our understanding of Angelo's mental pregnancy image: 'my sense breeds with it' is subtly qualified in the following scene by the sight of a very pregnant Juliet. Inner (mental) and outer (physical) action are in fact identical. The real pregnancy mirrors Angelo's embryonic image, which develops into a full-blown conception in Act II Scene iv. When he mentions 'the strong and swelling evil / Of my conception', the image works on several levels. It expresses his sexual longing as well as his thought-processes, and, of course, it is an image perfectly congruent with the pregnant atmosphere of the play. Angelo begs Isabella's understanding and sexual favour simultaneously in his proposition 'Plainly conceive, I love you' (II. iv. 140).

Angelo's conception is the desire to get Isabella to conceive by him. His plan fails. The Duke's re-entry into Vienna signals the start of Angelo's abortion process:

> This deed unshapes me quite; makes me
> Unpregnant and dull to all proceedings.
>
> (IV. iv. 18–19)

At the last, Isabella reluctantly pleads for Angelo's life, describing his thwarted wishes in abortion imagery:

> His act did not o'ertake his bad intent,
> And must be buried but as an intent
> That perish'd by the way.
>
> (v. i. 449–52)

We recall Angelo's words about the foetal evils in Vienna's womb, and his threat to abort them: 'ere they live, to end'. The final irony of *Measure for Measure* lies in Isabella's plea. Angelo's sexual hypocrisy, expressed in terms of pregnancy, is the great embryonic evil which perishes before birth. Paradoxically enough, this 'abortion' permits society to continue exercising its natural, life-producing urges.[23]

The Duke shares Angelo's fertile imagery. Disguised as a friar, he masterminds the bed-trick which foils Angelo's device. In effect, Angelo's wished-for birth, the concept which he hopes to realise, aborts in the face of the Duke's better conceived and executed idea. Both their concepts involve sexual intercourse, which results, if we may judge from Juliet's and Mrs Elbow's conditions, in pregnancy. Metaphor and reality thus mutually reinforce each other: the idea of getting someone pregnant is suggested in the imagery of pregnancy. In Act III scene i the Duke represents Mariana's misfortunes in images of abortion and hails his solution as a birth. According to his account of her troubles, the *de futuro* agreement between Angelo and Mariana was breached by the loss of her brother Frederick, 'who miscarried at sea' (III. i. 210). This miscarriage was disastrous for poor Mariana, for the sunken ship, which the Duke calls a 'perished vessel' (III. i. 217), claimed both her brother and her marriage dowry – 'the portion and sinew of her fortune' (III. i. 221–2). Angelo's subsequent betrayal of Mariana and blackmail of Isabella can both be redressed by Isabella's pretended submission and the substitution of Mariana for herself at an assigned rendezvous. The Duke's outline of the plot has bawdy overtones: 'The maid will I frame, and make fit for his attempt'

(III. i. 256–7).[24] The apparent inconsistency of these remarks with the Friar's habit seems perplexing, but the Duke goes on to explain the growth principle behind the plan:

> DUKE. . . . If you think well to *carry* this as you may, the doubleness of the benefit defends the deceit from reproof. What think you of it?
>
> ISABELLA. The *image* of it gives me *content* already, and I trust it will *grow* to a most *prosperous* perfection.
>
> DUKE. It lies much in your *holding up*.

> (III. i. 258–62, emphasis added)

This strangely stilted language perfectly expresses the embryonic quality of the idea. The terms I emphasise need no gloss. Isabella's chastity is preserved and Mariana's lost honour restored by Isabella's successful carriage and delivery of the Duke's 'baby'.

Throughout the play, the images of masculine potency metaphorically express man's power to act and emphasise the contrast between Angelo and the Duke. The Duke leaves Vienna, giving Angelo's deputation 'all the organs / Of our own power' (I. i. 20–1). As Angelo's perfidy becomes apparent, the Duke ironically remarks that 'his life is parallel'd / Even with the stroke and line of his great justice' (IV. ii. 77–8). We see this mighty stroke and line in action when Angelo responds to Isabella's appeal with sexual blackmail. The Duke's return to Vienna and his enforcement of justice testify to his greater potency. Angelo's image of Vienna-as-woman is insistently recalled in the Duke's description, replete with sexual innuendo, of his imminent return:

> by great injunctions I am bound
> To enter publicly. Him [Angelo] I'll desire
> To meet me at the consecrated fount
> A league below the city.

> (IV. iii. 95–8)

as in Friar Peter's equally suggestive revelation:

> The generous and gravest citizens
> Have hent the gates, and very near upon
> The Duke is ent'ring.

> (IV. iv. 13–15)

The Duke's penetration of the city limits, the opening gates, the holy fountain a league below, all contribute to a powerfully sexual atmosphere. His homecoming is metaphorically portrayed in terms of a vaginal penetration.[25] City is woman not only geographically but also in its feminine, subordinate relationship to the governor, implied in Lucio's use of imagery suggestive of male priapic dominance and feminine submission when discussing the nature of government early in the play:

> whether that the body public be
> A horse whereon the governor doth ride,
> Who, newly in the seat, that it may know
> He can command, lets it straight feel the spur;
> Whether the tyranny be in his place,
> Or in his eminence that fills it up,
> I stagger in.

> (I. i. 148–54)

A bewildered Angelo finally acknowledges the Duke's superior potency, directly relating civic administrative power to sexual prowess:

> These poor informal women are no more
> But instruments of some more mightier member
> That sets them on.

> (v. i. 235–7)

The hint of sexual potency is greatly amplified in the Duke's own proposition to Isabella at the end:

> I have a motion much imports your good;
> Whereto if you'll a willing ear incline,
> What's mine is yours, and what's yours is mine.

> (v. i. 532–4)

Against the Duke with his productive and important motion stands the sadly ineffective Angelo. In the last brazen moments of *Measure for Measure* (I cannot call them golden) we recall Lucio's description of him as 'a motion ungenerative' (III. ii. 108).

The source of Angelo's fatal attraction to Isabella lies in her appeal to his potency. A look at Shakespeare's ambiguous presentation of her will clarify this point. Claudio's entire description of Isabella's rhetorical qualities reeks with sexual innuendo:

> in her youth
> There is a prone and speechless dialect
> Such as move men; beside, she hath prosperous art
> When she will play with reason and discourse,
> And well she can persuade.
>
> (I. ii. 172–6)

In Act II scene ii, the persuasion scene, these techniques and abilities are brought into full play, and a detailed examination of the scene reveals quite clearly Isabella's role in Angelo's 'conception'.

Isabella's symbolism and direct utterances in Act II scene ii have a titillating ambiguity which provokes burning desire in Angelo. The strong sense of sexuality in this scene, despite the formal rhetorical overlay, is bolstered by Lucio's salacious asides, as he follows Isabella's sexual and rhetorical progress with Angelo, charting reactions in Angelo from indifference to a kind of orgasm. The Servant's announcement of Isabella's arrival contains a physical pun: 'Here is the sister of the man condemn'd,/Desires access to you' (II. ii. 18–19). She enters as 'a woeful suitor to your honour' (II. ii. 27), confessing herself 'at war 'twixt will and will not' (II. ii. 33).[26] The Provost quietly prays for good results: 'Heaven give thee moving graces!' (II. ii. 36). Already, the *double entendres* behind 'desires', 'access', 'suitor', 'will', 'moving' surround Isabella with a sexual aura which will magnetically draw Angelo to her. She presses on, arguing from basic ethics while Lucio scornfully mutters, 'You are too cold' (II. ii. 45, 56). Finally, she hits upon an apt phrase: 'I would to heaven I had your potency!' (II. ii. 67). Angelo is visibly moved, as Lucio notes in an extraordinarily bawdy line: 'Ay, touch him: there's the vein' (II. ii. 70). Isabella goes on to remark,

> it is excellent
> To have a giant's strength, but it is tyrannous
> To use it like a giant.
>
> (II. ii. 108–10)

She has already referred to 'the deputed sword, / The marshal's truncheon' (II. ii. 60–1), 'the top of judgement' (II. ii. 76), and now potency and the giant's strength. These phallic images constitute a 'penis-synomy',[27] catechised by Isabella, which provokes Angelo to irresistible desire. Isabella appeals to both his baser and better instincts; to his manhood as well as to his ethics. Given the context for double readings which has been established, Isabella's final trope resounds with devastatingly overt sexual symbolism:

> Merciful Heaven,
> Thou rather with thy sharp and sulphurous bolt
> Splits the unwedgeable and gnarled oak,
> Than the soft myrtle.
>
> (II. ii. 115–18)

She progresses from the bolt-split oak to identify man's one sure attribute: his 'glassy essence' (II. ii. 121). Certainly, it means 'soul', but, in light of all that has gone before, it also signifies 'sperm'. This touch wins Angelo over in more senses than one, as Lucio's aside amply demonstrates:

> O, to him, to him, wench! He will relent;
> He's coming: I perceive't.
>
> (II. ii. 125–6)

And in Act II scene iv, Angelo comes to a conception, the results of cerebration, but none the less as physically grounded as the real conception of the quiet and mysterious Juliet who crosses the stage in Act II scene iii.

Measure for Measure portrays the world realistically, devoid of illusions,[28] as its equivalent spiritual and physical terminology makes quite clear. We should do well to remember that *grace* and *justice*, two key concepts, first occur in the mouth of the irreverent Lucio (I. ii. 19–45); that the keywords of the play (including 'satisfaction', 'content', 'prosperous', 'head', 'bear', 'desire', 'crave', 'hang', 'point') have strong *double entendre*; and that the concept of *good* is rather dubiously related to sexual satisfaction throughout the play. How conscious or unconscious the characters are of their obscenity should not bother the broadminded reader or critic. Suffice it to say that the ubiquitous images of pregnancy and potency fittingly define the play's dramatic parameters and enhance its plot. There is enough leeway for actors and directors to play the dialogue both ways: *Measure for Measure* exhibits most richly, and most joyfully, Shakespeare's characteristic potential for antithetical readings. The acme of spirituality, the nadir of bawdy, are simultaneously reached, since the reader has the option of selecting either level or encompassing both in his own private interpretation.[29] And that interpretation may well differ at successive readings.[30] Just as Isabella moves and touches Angelo both spiritually and physically, so does the play move and touch us.

My reading of the play does not deny its spiritual side, and aims rather to applaud than question its style. Perhaps more than any other Shakespearian play, *Measure for Measure* is open to the highest and the lowest forms of commentary. There has certainly been plenty of niggling around in the middle on points of law, Elizabethan betrothals, plagues in London, and so on.[31] Even those critics who face the elements which so many of their colleagues have successfully avoided for years find themselves unable to handle the play's realism, and rather repelled by it. 'No healthy sexuality exists at the beginning of the play', writes Morris Partee.[32] Here is, says Lawrence Hyman, an 'unpleasant reciprocity between life and sin'.[33] Hilda Hulme once remarked that

> interpretation of Shakespearean innuendo, even when that innuendo is . . . organic, is not always acceptable. . . . There are many who would think it best not to give too much attention to this particular area of artistic language; we are perhaps not yet ready to give to it that degree of attention which Shakespeare gave.[34]

I cannot quite agree that interpretation of anything *organic* in Shakespeare is unacceptable. In order to understand the full implications of his drama, no critical tool should be ignored, and no textual stone left unturned. What is so unpleasant, so unhealthy, that Shakespeare uses the images of human sexuality and generation to express it?

It is in the coalescence of spiritual and physical that Shakespeare finds the essence of humanity: in man's ability to create a baby sexually and to conceive a brainchild cerebrally. *Measure for Measure* explores both these realities and makes them identical. The play stands central in Shakespeare's development of generation met-

aphor, combining figurative and actual pregnancy with a con-
sonance that colours all his subsequent work. The colour would first
be dark before brightening toward romance, for the very vulnerable
human condition which the problem plays explored led
Shakespeare to tragedy next. During the problem plays,
Shakespeare developed the ability to grapple with life and death as
realities rather than as dramatic conventions. From *Hamlet* to
Measure for Measure, here is a world of jesters' skulls and pregnant
bellies; a place where people are born, have children, and die. A
ripe environment for tragedy.

4 'This Monstrous Birth': The Tragedies

It should by now be obvious that we are no longer dealing with 'imagery', if we accept as the fundamental property of imagery the 'literal and concrete representation of a sensory experience or of an object that can be known by one or more of the senses'.[1] The types and uses of imagery in Shakespeare are so varied that they defy reductive analysis, forcing interpreters carefully to stake out the widest possible ground on which to base their studies:

> I use the term 'image' . . . as the only available word to cover every kind of simile, as well as every kind of what is really compressed simile – metaphor. I suggest that we divest our minds of the hint the term carries with it of visual image only, and think of it, for the present purpose, as connoting any and every imaginative picture or any other experience, drawn in every kind of way, which may have come to the poet, not only through any of his senses, but through his mind and emotions as well, and which he uses, in the forms of simile and metaphor in their widest sense, for purposes of analogy.[2]

Spurgeon's definition resembles critical legalese: every escape clause is carefully inserted. But, despite its enormous scope, this definition remains within the realms of language. Brian Vickers's all-encompassing classification includes elements which are patently not linguistic. His seven types of imagery are: thematic, situational, stage, atmospheric, subjective, objective, forensic (i.e. manipulative).[3] The sensitive scholar will no doubt recognise that what Vickers has called 'imagery' covers a good deal more ground than one expects. Actually, it covers everything.

The problem of imagery faces us as we approach the tragedies. What we are primarily concerned with is no longer an exclusively literary element. Shakespeare's tragedies move, as has been noted in another context, 'beyond the level of explicitness'.[4] And it is not singly word, action, staging, character definition, plot or theme that carries us into this difficult territory: it is a combination of all these elements. Once it had encompassed the realities of birth and death in his problem plays, Shakespeare's technique became less stylised and far more intuitive. His thought (the Aristotelian *dianoia*) is so highly condensed that one cannot easily extract choice quotations or incidents to support interpretations. Perhaps that is why some scholars feel constrained to quote virtually the whole play or give plot summaries when discussing them.[5] Critics speak of the 'world' or 'universe' of each tragedy,[6] and it is almost impossible to state where the bourns between various dramatic functions lie. Finally, imagery appears to be everything we see or hear in the play, whose sum total contributes to that image we make for ourselves.

Those metaphors which flared into brilliance at certain points in Shakespeare's early plays now become an integral part of his dramaturgy, deeply embedded in the linguistic and conceptual fabric of the plays. The advance from *Love's Labour's Lost*, for example, is tremendous. There, as in most of his early work, Shakespeare's characters are delightfully aware of their clever double meanings. Or, at least, Shakespeare has them express themselves in such a manner that we are delightfully aware. The language is in a state of conscious experimentation and trial. In the great tragedies, we see the same semantic brilliance as in the early plays, but its use is far more sustained and self-conscious. Shakespeare deploys his key contrasting images, instinctively, invisibly. So that, for instance, when we hear such an exchange as

DOCTOR. You see her eyes are open.
GENTLEWOMAN. Ay, but their sense are shut.

(*Macbeth*, v. i. 28–9)

we may register the open/closed door imagery as apposite and entertaining, but we probably fail to make the connection between Lady Macbeth's eyes, open or shut, and the open doors of Duncan's bedroom after his murder, or the opening of the great Hell-gate to Macbeth's castle by the Porter as the awful news is announced. Actors playing the Doctor and Gentlewoman would be unwise to stress the metaphor in their readings. Typically of Shakespeare's tragedies, texture, rather than detail, washes over the reader. Or rather, a texture composed of myriads of inseparable tiny details.

For any critic whose work involves tangible, historical evidence, the task of interpretational proof is relatively easy. The image-oriented critic, who must rely on those intangible qualities of text which provoke instinctual response in the reader, faces a much harder question, namely: 'How do you prove a feeling?' In this chapter I shall consider the mature tragedies first as a group, and then examine *Othello*, *King Lear* and *Macbeth* individually. I hope finally to show how the handling of themes and images of motherhood in Shakespeare's late tragedies, *Timon of Athens*, *Antony and Cleopatra*, *Coriolanus*, point us toward his last plays. I share Dr Hulme's position on interpretational proof: any reader convinced by the readings I offer should ask himself exactly what he has allowed to convince him, and how he would convince others of the validity of those interpretations.[7] Let me add that, if the stylistic critic should be accused of woolliness by his more precisely minded peers, it is perhaps because he seeks to unravel the threads of an unbreachable totality.

The emphasis on the child's role in the tragic plots was an inevitable one for Shakespeare, since the child–parent relationship had always fascinated him. We find it throughout the comedies: in *The Two Gentlemen of Verona* (Silvia and the Duke of Milan; Proteus and Antonio), *Love's Labour's Lost* (the Princess returns home for her father's funeral), *The Taming of the Shrew* (Katherina, Bianca and Baptista; Tranio and Vincentio), *A Midsummer Night's Dream* (Hermia and Egeus), *Much Ado About Nothing* (Hero and Leonato), and *As You Like It* (Celia and Duke Frederick). In almost all these plots, we do not relate to the children as children, but rather as young adults. Prior to the great tragedies, the filial relationships, although ubiquitous, are downplayed, and do not become points of central conflict. Sometimes this is accomplished by keeping the father offstage and never introducing him into the drama (*Love's Labour's Lost*), or by replacing the parental–filial conflict with a lovers' conflict (*The Taming of the Shrew*), or by keeping the scenes of conflict at a minimum and basically comic in tone (*As You Like It*, *A Midsummer Night's Dream*), or by restricting the child–parent encounters to stock dramatic situations, such as the recognition scenes in *The Taming of the Shrew* and *The Comedy of Errors*. At all events, the parent–child conflict does not seriously impinge upon us in the comedies. We are more concerned with the children *qua* young lovers, than *qua* children. The notable exception is *Romeo and Juliet*. Here the filial relationship is crucial – and proves tragic.

After the problem plays, which deal with procreative sex, come the tragedies, where the transition from lovers to families is accomplished. The dramatic focus now shifts onto children, the issue of marriage. This new emphasis is entirely to be expected in a man of middle age, since

> it would hardly be surprising if thoughts of generation and death should not absorb a playwright approaching forty, since by that age a man sees children, not merely as infants, but as adult replacements for the present generation.[8]

Having explored in *Measure for Measure* the relationship between sex and the law, Shakespeare now turned his attention to the nature of marriage. *The Merry Wives of Windsor* has a comic plot about a villain falsely persuading a man of his wife's infidelity. *Othello*, written a few years later, resurrects the same theme and gives it a tragic perspective. In *Othello*, however, the wife is an eloped child. The figure of the child becomes increasingly important in the mature tragedies. The dramatic impetus for *Lear* is the filial rejection scene, and *Macbeth*'s nemesis is the caesarian-born child, who has somehow escaped his murdering hands. In *Macbeth*, the most genealogical of the tragedies, the concern with entire family lines prepares us for the familial disunion and reunion of the last plays.

The agony, at once spiritual and physical, of Angelo paved the way for a use of bawdy quite distinct from that in Shakespeare's comedies. In the tragedies, more than in his preceding dramas, Shakespeare's generation metaphor is closely allied to his characters' sexuality. Without wishing to indulge in psychoanalytical criticism any earlier than necessary, I think one may safely say that we are tempted to guess at the tragic characters' sexual landscape by a careful look at the generation imagery they use in spiritual contexts. That is to say, the language in which they cast their thought-processes sheds interesting light on their sexual nature. One is more fascinated by the sexuality of Othello, Iago, Lady Macbeth, than by that of Bottom, Benedick, Bianca, despite the more heavy-handed use of bawdy language in the comedies. The obvious bawdy of Launce in *The Two Gentlemen of Verona* has no significance beyond its immediate, obscene appeal. By contrast, the birth imagery of Iago, formulating his fiction, invites speculation as to his sexual character. Is he impotent? Homosexual? He does not say. But his richly sexual idiom is loaded with hints.

From what we have seen in the problem plays, we can expect the language of generation to occupy an important place in the tragedies. The problem plays opened up for Shakespeare the vast punning potential of words such as 'pregnant', 'conception', and all their qualifiers, synonyms and opposites. In the tragedies, the imagery of generation is the supreme indicator of a character's creativity. Whether the universe it circumscribes is good or evil does not lessen its force. With the tragedies, Shakespeare reaches the limits of language. The theme is verbal persuasion; the receptive organ the ear. We are a long way from the deceived eyes of the comedies. Toward the end of his tragic period, Shakespeare turned increasingly to stage-image, emblem and icon, presentational devices which revealed his ideas 'more pregnantly than words'.[9]

But in Shakespeare's mature tragedies it is words, the conveyers of thought, which have power to impregnate and fertilise. Nowhere is this more clearly apparent than in *Othello*, the tragedy of the manipulated man. Iago, the manipulator *par excellence*, ranks as a character extraordinarily sensitive to the creative process. As far his relationship with Othello goes, most critics have noticed the change in Othello's rhetoric after the temptation scene (III. iii). His altered vocabulary is an external manifestation of his changed mind, sequent to Iago's influence. Let us consider Iago's creativity and Othello's altered rhetoric in terms of the imagery of generation in which Iago conceives his brainchild, and which becomes a feature of Othello's language as soon as he is convinced of Iago's credibility.

In a manner typical of Shakespeare's tragic protagonists, Iago often uses a verbal image that later manifests itself in reality. Perhaps, indeed, this dramatic trait is 'Shakespeare's way of indicating that it is the individual himself who arranges his own fate. . . . In such parallel phenomena the action occurs on two planes: first, on the psychic plane, then later as an external event.'[10] In Act I scene iii, Iago's famous garden speech to Roderigo seems designed to rouse himself as well as Roderigo to action. He concludes his remarks with the darkly portentous dictum, 'There are many events in the womb of time which will be delivered' (I. iii. 376–8). Shortly after Roderigo's exit, Iago himself comes into actual contact with one of these embryonic events as he conceives the idea of abusing Othello's credulity:

I have't. It is engend'red. Hell and night
Must bring this monstrous birth to the world's light.

(I. iii. 409–10)

The image which describes Iago's experience is identical with the image he had used purely as metaphor. In this scene, then, the tone of Iago's theoretical advice to Roderigo determines the context in which he views his own subsequent experience. And, by extension, the context in which the audience must view the burgeoning thought and ripening action of *Othello*.

The next scene shows Iago again using birth-imagery as he constructs a ludic 'argument' – this time in doggerel verse. Again, the same image is used to express the real situation shortly afterwards. Upon arrival at Cyprus, Desdemona asks him to write something in her praise. After a modest delay, Iago prefaces his obscene doggerel with 'my Muse labours, / And thus she is deliver'd' (II. i. 128–9). As it happens, Desdemona does not think much of Iago's brainchild. She dismisses his barbed final volta as a 'most lame and impotent conclusion' (II. i. 162), a singularly unfortunate choice of words which strikes right at the heart of Iago's sexual insecurity. We already know that Iago suspects Othello of adultery with his wife, Emilia. But the little failure to satisfy Desdemona does not matter much, since Iago is bent on proving his fertility in other ways. As in the exchange with Roderigo in Act I scene iii, the figurative language which he uses in playing 'creative' provides him with the idiom to develop his idea and persuade others of its plausibility. Like the invention of his little ballad, Iago's invention of the slander on Cassio is also a pregnancy. In these words, he sets about convincing Roderigo:

> nature will . . . compel her to some second choice. Now, sir, this granted, – as it is a most *pregnant* and unforc'd position – who stands so eminent in the degree of this fortune as Cassio does? (II. i. 236–41, emphasis added)

Iago's birth-imagery both precedes and accompanies his creative process.[11] He rehearses it in play and then employs it in earnest. The origin of his fiction and his first try at persuasion are as much births as his stylised rhetoric and poetry-making.

Iago seeks to duplicate in his victims exactly what he has himself experienced: the materialisation of an idea.[12] His creativity, like the poet's, is absolute. Let us pause here to recall Puttenham's description of the poet's mental activity in *The Arte of English Poesie* (1589). The kinship with Iago's creativity is self-explanatory:

> A Poet is as much to say as a maker. . . . Such as . . . we may say of God; who without any travell to his divine imagination made all the world of nought, nor also by any paterne or mould. . . . Even so the very Poet makes and contrives out of his own braine both the verse and matter of his poeme.[13]

Iago's generative processes, whether on the ludic or serious level, prefigure the mental impregnation of Othello. As Wolfgang Clemen perceptively observes, Iago 'aims to implant in the minds of his victims a conceit which will gradually assume gigantic proportions'.[14] The very act of impregnation. It is noteworthy that Iago more or less fails with Roderigo in Act II scene i because he talks too much. He does not repeat the mistake. Deceiving Othello is a much easier business: Iago just lets Othello talk himself into suspicion.

In Act III scene iii, the 'temptation scene', then, Othello really tempts himself. His mere observation of Iago is enough to initiate his own misconception. What principally impresses Othello about Iago's general bearing is his pregnant pause, his refusal to disclose his inner thought:

> By heaven, he echoes me,
> As if there were some monster in his thought
> Too hideous to be shown.
>
> (III. iii. 106–8)

And, in a strange echo of the 'purse' motif, we learn that this monster is a conceit which is readily apparent in Iago's general demeanour. Othello fatally misconstrues Iago's facial attitude in his fascination:

> when I told thee he [Cassio] was of my counsel
> In my whole course of wooing, thou criedst, 'Indeed!'
> And didst contract and *purse* thy brow together,
> As if thou then hadst shut up in thy brain
> Some horrible conceit.
>
> (III. iii. 111–15, emphasis added)

The verb 'purse' is of paramount importance. In his *Anatomie of the Bodie of Man* (1548; 2nd edn 1577), Thomas Vicary, Sergeant Surgeon to Henry VIII, Edward VI, Mary and Elizabeth I, compares the womb, sealed at one end, to a purse: 'The necke . . . in her concavitie hath many involutions and pleates, joyned together in the maner of Rose leaves before they be fully spread or ripe, and so they be shut togeather as a Purse mouth.'[15] To Othello's view, Iago's brainchild, his 'conceit', appears tantalisingly 'shut up' within his womblike, purselike brain. The verb 'purse' also recalls to us Iago's early advice to Roderigo: 'Put money in thy purse' (I. ii. 344). This axiom is generally interpreted as indicative of Iago's general opportunism. However, this new usage, coupled with Vicary's simile, makes possible an alternative gloss for the line: 'impregnate yourself with productive concepts'. As we know, Iago is very concerned with impregnating himself with such conceits. And now, in Act III scene iii, he nonchalantly confesses to Othello, 'Who steals my purse steals trash; 'tis something, nothing' (III. iii. 157). The paradoxical 'something, nothing' alerts us to the association with the feminine machinery of reproduction; we recall Queen Isabel fainting and shrinking with her heavy nothings, for example. By the middle of the scene, Othello has 'stolen' Iago's purse of thoughts to the extent that his own brows contract in painful support of the trashy thoughts in his head. Desdemona finds him in visible agony, pursing his brows just as Iago did earlier in the scene:

DESDEMONA. Why do you speak so faintly?
  Are you not well?
OTHELLO. I have a pain upon my forehead here.

(III. iii. 282–4)[16]

Iago succeeds with Othello because he allows him to create an imaginary situation entirely for himself by picking up on his sparse hints – in a sense, by stealing his purse. Act III scene iii thematically ties together the images of birth and filled purses in the transferral of the pursed brow, bulging with conceit, from Iago to Othello.

From this point on the birth-imagery refers to Othello's embryonic ideas rather than Iago's. In effect, Iago has impregnated Othello with a false, non-existent reality; the two men are thus psychosexually interlinked.[17] The principal characters to feel the full physical and emotional impact of Othello's changed state are

Desdemona and her maid, Emilia. Both mystified, they dimly divine Othello's strange behaviour in the context of mental pregnancy. Desdemona wonders what 'unhatch'd practice / Made demonstrable here in Cyprus to him' (III. iv. 141–2) has disturbed Othello. The women continue their dialogue, extending the pun on 'unhatch'd':

> EMILIA. Pray Heaven it be state-matters, as you think,
>   And no *conception* nor no jealous toy
>   Concerning you.
> DESDEMONA. Alas the day! I never gave him cause.
> EMILIA. But jealous souls will not be answer'd so;
>   They are not ever jealous for the cause,
>   But jealous for they're jealous. It is a monster
>   *Begot* upon itself, *born* on itself.
>
> (III. iv. 155–62, emphasis added)

In Emilia's last two lines, the auto-impregnation aspect emerges clearly enough. A singular irony then appears in Othello's dismissal of Emilia at the beginning of the 'whorehouse' scene, Act IV scene ii: 'Leave procreants alone' (IV. ii. 28). 'Procreants' has two senses here: first, it functions as a basic description of people indulging in generative sex at its most instinctive and animal level; and secondly, more sophisticatedly, it reflects the mental state of Othello, procreating his disastrous conception. Othello proceeds to castigate Desdemona mercilessly. The first line after his exit, from a bewildered Emilia, is 'Alas, what does this gentleman conceive?' (IV. ii. 94), and the substantiality of Othello's delusion is beautifully expressed in her outburst, ironically directed to the impregnator Iago, 'What place? what time? what *form*? what likelihood?' (IV. ii. 138, emphasis added)

Othello has conceived what Hamlet believed himself unpregnant of: a *cause*. His run-up to Desdemona's murder horribly travesties the moment before birth:

> confess thee freely of thy sin;
> For to deny each article with oath
> Cannot remove nor choke the strong conception
> That I do groan withal.
>
> (V. ii. 53–6)

The birth by murder accomplished, Othello gradually returns to his old rhetorical patterns and 'to a hardened kind of knowing'.[18] But, if Othello's lapsarian course has paralleled Adam's as closely as this implies, then we can expect Iago to bear some similarity to the first serpent. Indeed, he bleeds, and does not die. But, more than this, Iago's entire technique of impregnating his victims with pretended and non-existent reality anticipates the fertile, fatal persuasiveness of Milton's Satan:

> He ended, and his words replete with guile
> Into her heart too easie entrance won;
> Fixt on the Fruit she gaz'd, which to behold
> Might tempt alone, and in her ears the sound
> Yet rung of his perswasive words, *impregned*
> With Reason, to her seeming, and with truth.[19]

Eve's aural impregnation by Satan was the dark reverse of a tradition which upheld belief in the *conceptio per aurem* of Mary. This is a favourite motif in mediaeval Annunciation scenes. Mary sits or stands, rapt or attentive, sometimes with her back to the announcing angel. Above her head the thought of Christ floats as a dove, a beam of light, or the baby figure itself. In some paintings, the baby may be seen in Mary's womb even as the angel announces her eventual pregnancy.[20]

Renaissance poets supposed themselves equally receptive and capable of being similarly 'in-spired', i.e. having the divine *pneuma* blown into them. Spenser's invocation on behalf of his inner ear ('give me words') clearly assigns to God the role of masculine impregnator shedding vital juices into the poet's waiting mind. The all-too-human functions of orgasm and pregnancy are mystically elevated to a divine level:

> Yet o most blessed Spirit, pure lamp of light,
> Eternall Spring of grace and wisedome trew,
> Vouchsafe to shed into my barren spright
> Some little drop of thy celestial dew,
> That may my rymes with sweet infuse enbrew,
> And give me words equall unto my thought,
> To tell the marveiles by thy mercie wrought.[21]

Even this resoundingly paternalistic God enjoys a certain hermaphroditic character. Spenser later mentions that God is 'pregnant still with powerful grace',[22] loving to reproduce himself in mankind. The feminine metaphor provided ultimate expression of divine or human creativity. Pregnancy encompassed the ability to grasp and recognise cosmic significances, whether for good or evil. In imitation of a fertile God, the pregnant poet would turn embryonic ideas into a literary creation;[23] and every man would convert thought to action, ever inspiring himself and others to perceive, conceive and act.

Shakespeare's tragic heroes, from Hamlet to Coriolanus, are convinced of the importance of living a fertile, productive life. The tragedies naturally present a pessimistic outlook. As in the comedies, and increasingly so, the generative function of the brain receiving information, piecing it together, nurturing it and 'delivering' it out again through action is all-important. The satanic side of the aural impregnation archetype predominates. The hearing faculty is linked with fatality, death, disaster. Tragic mishearings replace to a large extent the optical errors of the comedies, and death, not life, enters by way of the ear. In the tragedies, where the thought-to-action pattern is central, the aural impregnation motif constantly recurs: old Hamlet dies when Claudius pours poison in his ears, and his report urges young Hamlet to action; Othello acts upon the aural impregnation by Iago; Lady Macbeth hisses Macbeth's speedy return so that she may pour her spirits in his ear.

Aural impregnation of course requires the presence of two people – a speaker and a listener. But cerebral auto-impregnation (having an idea on one's own) is quite another thing. As we saw with *Hamlet*, and in Iago, pregnancy denotes fertility in oneself as well as receptivity and suggestibility to the impregnating ideas of others. Throughout Shakespeare's tragedies, imagery of generation appropriately accompanies the birthing of ideas, projects, actions. This usage was first employed by Shakespeare as early as *Love's Labour's Lost*. His protagonists have characteristically viewed their most creative endeavours, their greatest strivings, in terms of generation. This metaphor now assumes an added dimension because of actual generation in the tragedies: the increased prominence of children amplifies our frame of reference and adds subtle shadings and ironies. All these factors work together to colour the thought and action of Shakespeare's characters in tragic crisis.

In *King Lear*, which followed *Othello*, the reality of generation predominates. The play explores the generation gap and filial–

parental relationships, but, as is the case with most of the dramatic elements in *Lear*, the generation metaphor is so highly complex and diffuse that any analysis risks making nonsense of the drama. However, typically of Shakespeare, the imagery is powerful, though scattered, occurring at certain key moments of both action and theme, and fulfilling functions similar to those we have already observed in other plays.

Lear's remark to Kent 'Thou but rememb'rest me of mine own conception' (I. iv. 72–3) is significant indeed. It is uttered at the beginning of his downward swing: he has realised that all is not as it should be in his relationship with Goneril. How appropriate that Lear's epiphanic moment of understanding his child's perfidy should centre on the word 'conception', which unites the two senses of 'child' and 'understanding' or 'thought'. During the remainder of this scene, the Fool brings Lear's situation fully home to him in a bombardment of obscene riddles and fertility symbols (the egg, the crown). And, after Goneril's cruelty establishes her disloyalty, Lear curses her in her womb, the seat of generation:

> Hear, Nature! hear, dear goddess, hear!
> Suspend thy purpose, if thou didst intend
> To make this creature fruitful!
> Into her womb convey sterility!
> Dry up in her the organs of increase,
> And from her derogate body never spring
> A babe to honour her!

(I. iv. 297–303)

In effect, Lear, having had his own 'conception' (= 'thought') about his 'conception' (= 'child') proved beyond doubt by her actions, curses her in regard to any of her future conceptions (procreative powers). The metaphorical and the actual are homogenised.

In the case of *King Lear*, puns involving a generation metaphor are crucial to the play's thought.[24] First, they underscore the plot, which deals with generation. Secondly, they constitute an ironic reversal, since they occur most often in the mouths of the children and not of the fathers, as might be more reasonably expected. It is fitting that Lear should curse Goneril in her womb, since she has already stated her intention to 'breed from hence occasions . . . / That I may speak' (I. iii. 24–5). Lear feels his rising melancholy, induced by Goneril's behaviour, as 'this *mother* [that] swells up toward my heart!' (II. iv. 56, emphasis added),[25] and uses the same metaphor when putting an imaginary Regan on trial: 'Then let them anatomize Regan; see what breeds about her heart' (III. iv. 80–1). The same metaphor also conveys the Gloucester children's creativity. The old Earl, unable to believe Edgar capable of the kind of treachery of which Edmund falsely accuses him, exclaims, 'My son Edgar! Had he a hand to write this? a heart and brain to breed it in?' (I. ii. 59–61), and fugitive Edgar, disguised as poor Tom, describes himself as 'pregnant to good pity' (IV. vi. 227). In *King Lear and the Gods*, William Elton draws an interesting distinction between the connotations of generation imagery for Edgar and for Goneril and Regan: 'Where Edgar can be "pregnant to good pity", sympathy being a creative force, the evil sisters can only . . . labor in sterile activity, bringing forth chaos.'[26] In terms of this contrast, we see how skilfully Shakespeare has employed the iterative imagery of pregnancy to delineate character and motivation.

The most sustained generation metaphor in *King Lear* belongs to Edmund and also charts the development of his relationship with Goneril. That Edmund should express himself and his aspirations in this way is singularly appropriate, since the circumstances of his own birth provide the base matter for the infamous pun Gloucester makes in the first scene:

> KENT. I cannot conceive you.
> GLOUCESTER. Sir, this young fellow's mother could; whereupon she grew round-womb'd, and had, indeed, sir, a son for her cradle ere she had a husband for her bed.
>
> (I. i. 12–16)

The natural, bubbling spontaneity associated with Shakespeare's 'bastard' characters attaches to Edmund. Seething under the social stigma of his illegitimate birth, he uses verbs of procreation and growth to describe his evil creativity:

> if this letter speed
> And my invention *thrive*, Edmund the base
> Shall top th' legitimate. I *grow*; I *prosper*.
>
> (I. ii. 19–21, emphasis added)[27]

Stabbing himself to frame Edgar, he conjectures, 'Some blood drawn on me would beget opinion / Of my more fierce endeavour' (II. i. 35–6). In the letter which he forges, purporting to come from Edgar, Edmund also uses 'pregnant', although in a very different way from Edgar's 'pregnant to good pity':

> thou must make a dullard of the world
> If they not thought the profits of my death
> Were very pregnant and potential spurs
> To make thee seek it.

(II. i. 76–9)

Obliquely offering herself to Edmund, Goneril bids him, 'Conceive, and fare thee well' (IV. ii. 24); and, plotting Albany's death, she writes, 'time and place will be fruitfully offer'd' (IV. vi. 269–70). Edmund never receives the letter, since Oswald is waylaid by Edgar and killed. Regan speaks with unconscious irony when she surmises, 'Our sister's man is certainly miscarried' (V. i. 5).

The inventiveness of the evil children in *King Lear* finds expression in generation metaphor and wordplay, which counterpoint the actual generation of the plot. Goneril, Regan and Edmund are not 'incapable of "creative" imagery',[28] since one of their leading images is the primary image of creation. That the universe they seek to establish is evil is consonant with the tragic nature of the play. Erroneously believing himself thwarted in his desire to 'set my rest / On her [Cordelia's] kind nursery' (I. i. 125–6), Lear over-hastily exposes himself to the perverted maternal instincts of Goneril and Regan. Like Edmund, they hatch and breed their plans. Tonal consistency is maintained by the Fool's fertile symbols and riddles, and Lear thunders over the storm for an end to the human generative process: 'Crack nature's moulds, all germens spill at once / That makes ingrateful man!' (III. ii. 8–9). Lear's subsequent sexual nausea, which has been the object of much speculation, should not come as too much of a surprise. If his foul language does ultimately plummet from the sky and aim below the female waist, the denouncement of sexual pleasure condemns the only source of generation man really knows.[29]

In *Macbeth*, as in *King Lear*, actual and metaphorical generation permeate the action and language of the play. The points made in Cleanth Brooks's seminal study 'The Naked Babe and the Cloak of Manliness'[30] are, I think, generally accepted today, despite the furious objections made by some critics when his essay was first published.[31] Brooks mainly sought to establish the pre-eminence of child symbolism in *Macbeth*. He demonstrated that the child, appearing in language, in plot, and onstage, signifies both the 'unpredictable future' and 'human compassion'.[32] As a growth symbol, the child is supplemented by plant imagery. Brooks also expanded Spurgeon's interpretation of the clothes symbolism in the play,[33] tying it in with themes of hypocrisy, maturity and manhood. He cleverly located a connection between the play's growth symbols and wardrobe imagery in the Birnam-Wood-to-Dunsinane camouflage, which unites plant symbolism with clothes symbolism.[34]

However, the children and other growth-figures in *Macbeth* do not only symbolise the future and compassion – they are also metaphors for physical and mental fertility. Outside Macbeth's castle, martlets breed. Inside is hell, where Lady Macbeth unsexes herself, to fit herself for murder. Macbeth, consumed by self-love and hated by Hecate for it,[35] is adept at making images of death (I. iii. 96–7); this particular talent opens the way for his political advancement. With his sexuality and resolve constantly in question, and with his innermost doubts reinforced by Lady Macbeth's rhetoric[36] and the witches' sexual ambiguity,[37] Macbeth bumbles and fumbles his way to the top, only to find himself there determining that

> From this moment
> The very firstlings of my heart shall be
> The firstlings of my hand.
>
> (IV. i. 146–8)

The use of 'firstlings' (= 'first-born children') presents a paradox. Macbeth's brainchildren translate themselves into murderous acts, which manifest his mental sterility.[38] Tormented by the vision of Banquo's children striding from the future into the present to claim their inheritance, Macbeth himself has no horizon. To him, life is meaningless, a succession of tedious, barren tomorrows creeping inconsequentially toward the grave.

It is now a critical commonplace to perceive *Macbeth* as a play which deals with birth on various levels. In fact, 'the conception and birth of criminality' is seen as a central theme by Michael J. B. Allen. In an illuminating article on 'Macbeth's Genial Porter' Allen summons a wealth of evidence, garnered from etymology, mythology and folklore, to show the association of the porter-figure with the 'genius' of fifteenth- and sixteenth-century Latin mythologies. Etymologically, Allen bases his arguments on the 'rich complex of meanings signalled by the Latin word *gero*, to bear', and detects in the definitions of Latin equivalents for 'porter' and 'genius' a 'significant overlapping in the area of literal and metaphorical children'. All of this implicitly supports Brooks and has further profound implications for our understanding of *Macbeth*. Allen demonstrates that the three associations of the evil genius – with pregnancy, with man's higher destiny, and with the final betrayal of man's soul – cohere in the character of Macbeth's Porter. Allen's foray into the etymology and genealogy of the Porter clarifies the Porter's relationship to Macbeth[39] and elucidates the Porter's scene (II. iii). However, the scope of his article did not permit Professor Allen fully· to explore the implications of the definitions and cognates he provides. A semantic investigation not only completes our understanding of 'the scene's ironies and pseudo-comedy'[40] but also reveals further interesting permutations on the theme of birth in the play.

A relationship of the root syllable, 'port-', with pregnancy is urged in Thomas Raynalde's enumeration of the female reproductive system in *The Byrth of Mankynde, otherwyse named The Womans Booke* (1560):

> The necke of thys Wombe, otherwyse called the Womans privitie, we wyll call the wombe passage, or the privie passage: in Latine *Cervex uteri, & pudendum muliebre*; the extreme end, or the first entraunce of this privie or wombe passage, ye shall name the passage port: for because that it is the porte gate, or entraunce of that passage, or way into the wombe or matrix: in Latine, *Vulva*.[41]

Shakespeare himself identifies 'port-' with birth in Pericles's words to Marina, born upon a tempestuous sea: 'Thy loss is more than can thy portage quit' (*Pericles*, III. i. 35).

The primary sense of the verb 'port' is 'to carry' or 'to bear,' and throughout *Macbeth* things are carried or borne. Lady Macbeth counsels her husband to 'bear welcome in your eye' (I. v. 65) to Duncan, and, after Duncan's inhospitable murder, to 'go carry' (II. ii. 49) the daggers back to his chamber, so that the grooms may 'bear the guilt' (I. vii. 71) as originally planned. Macbeth, pondering the murder, believes that 'Duncan hath borne his faculties so meek'(I. vii. 17). In an apparent faulty parallel, Macbeth unites the two offices of a porter – gatekeeper and carrier[42] – and feels that he should 'against his murderer shut the door, / Not bear the knife myself' (I. vii. 15–16). The missing link which connects the otherwise inexplicably juxtaposed 'shut the door' with 'bear' is the hidden root 'port'. Hecate deplores her exclusion from the witches' plans:

> I, the mistress of your charms,
> The close contriver of all harms,
> Was never called to bear my part.
>
> (III. v. 6–8)

She prophesies that Macbeth will 'bear / His hopes 'bove wisdom, grace, and fear' (III. v. 29–30). And so we find Lennox suspiciously observing that 'things have been strangely borne', and that Macbeth 'has borne all things well' (III. vi. 3, 17). Macbeth is distraught to see that Banquo's descendants 'twofold balls and treble sceptres carry' (IV. i. 121). Ross, bringing Macduff the tragic news of his family's murder, is upset about 'the tidings, / Which I have heavily borne' (IV. iii. 181–2). Finally, the retributive stratagem includes the keyword 'bear': 'Let every soldier hew him down a bough / And bear't before him' (V. iv. 4–5). In his ultimate fight with Macduff, Macbeth uses the verb in two etymologically related forms, uniting the themes of fate and childbirth in his over-confident assertion 'I bear a charmed life, which must not yield / To one of woman born' (V. viii. 12–13).

What do we make of all these bearings, these 'portings', in the play? First, I think, they support the theme of childbirth, since 'bear' constitutes the experience of pregnancy. *Macbeth* inhabits a world where 'each minute teems' a new bit of information (IV. iii. 176), where events are 'new hatch'd to th' woeful time' (II. iii. 64), where projects are 'firstlings' (IV. i. 147–8), and Scotland itself a grieving mother (IV. iii). If we accept Cleanth Brooks's interpretation of the immanent child in Macbeth as symbolising the future, then we must take the verb 'bear' to denote symbolically the pregnant expectancy of the future. Secondly, 'bear' has a heavy ethical connotation in the play: one bears sin, or the awareness of it. A confused Macduff tells the equivocating Malcolm that his sins are 'portable' (IV. iii. 89).[43] Conversely, rectitude may be borne as well. In this sense, the action whereby Malcolm's soldiers bear Birnam

Wood to Dunsinane makes the army a large collective 'porter' rising against the porter Macbeth, who overweeningly bears his hopes too high.

The inclusion of the keyword 'bear' in the inception of the Birnam Wood plan (v. iv. 4–7) gives the manoeuvre another dimension, linking it with the unified growth (plants) and clothes symbols perceived by Brooks. The connection between 'bear' and growth is clear enough. But how are 'bear' and clothes related? Again, we turn to the hidden root 'port', and discover another shade of meaning: deportment, the manner in which one bears or carries oneself. Birnam Wood is borne and worn. In effect, Shakespeare puns on a concealed bivalent root,[44] thus forging a semantic as well as episodic link between growth and wardrobe imagery. This connection between 'port' and clothing also informs Lady Macbeth's notorious mixed metaphor, which had perplexed Brooks.[45] She goads Macbeth, 'Was the hope drunk/Wherein you dress'd yourself?' (I. vii. 35–6). 'Dress'd' means 'comported' here. Moreover, Lady Macbeth continues with 'Hath it slept since?' (I. vii. 36), paralleling the drunken Porter's description of drink, which has the effect of equivocating man 'in a sleep' (II. iii. 39–40). Lady Macbeth's taunts confirm the ties between Macbeth and the Porter and connect the Porter to the major verbal images of the play.

Shakespeare's associative train has not yet ground to a halt. Let us consider even more closely the words in which the Birnam Wood manoeuvre is formulated:

> Let every soldier hew him down a bough
> And bear't before him; thereby shall we shadow
> The numbers of our host and make discovery
> Err in report of us.

> (v. iv. 4–7)

Malcolm's strategy involves a compound verb from the root 'port': 'report'. It should hardly be necessary to remark the significance of reports in *Macbeth*. Information is carried around, reported and misreported. Indeed, 'report' is a minor keyword, representing the sum of all the voices, human, symbolic, inanimate, and personified, which cry throughout the play. Examples of reportage in *Macbeth* abound. Duncan listens to the bloody Captain's battle report (I. ii). Malcolm has spoken with one who reported the purity of Cawdor's

death (i. iv). Macbeth writes to his wife of the weird sisters: 'I have
learn'd by the perfect'st report, they have more in them than mortal
knowledge' (i. v. 2–4). This report will finally undo him.

By stressing equivocation, the play continually emphasises the
importance of substantiated or confirmed reports. The Doctor
confesses that he perceives no truth in the Gentlewoman's report
(v. i. 2), and consequently she declines to report (v. i. 16) Lady
Macbeth's utterances in the absence of a witness 'to confirm my
speech' (v. i. 20–1). As Birnam Wood advances, Macbeth orders,
'Bring me no more reports: let them fly all' (v. iii. 1), and Seyton
conveys the news of the army's arrival with 'All is confirm'd, my
lord, which was reported' (v. iii. 30–1). This dismal news completes
the tragically long leap from the enticing testimony of the witches
(i. iii). Lady Macbeth's ecstatic response to Macbeth's letters was
significant:

> Thy letters have transported me beyond
> This ignorant present, and I feel now
> The future in the instant.

> (i. v. 57–9)

In a sense, Lady Macbeth, exultant over Macbeth's report of things
to come, has been prematurely carried over – 'transported' – into
the future. Again, the root 'port' accompanies a thematic statement,
for the concept of immediate futurity juxtaposed with a port
('carry') verb recalls the birth theme, supporting Brooks's con-
tention that the symbolical child of Macbeth represents the
future.

Yet another refinement of the concept 'carry' or 'bear' linked
with prematurity prefaces Macbeth's final battle:

> Make all our trumpets speak; give them all breath,
> Those clamorous harbingers of blood and death.

> (v. vi. 9–10)

The word 'harbinger', which means 'forerunner' or 'early deliverer
of news', is ironically used here. It derives from Old French
herbergere, 'one who provides shelter or lodgings', and relates to Old
High German and Old Low German *heriberga*, literally 'shelter for
an army'.[46] The term had not quite lost its militaristic overtones in

Macbeth, as we see from its use in a significantly different context earlier in the play. Macbeth runs on ahead of the army to alert Lady Macbeth to Duncan's arrival:

> I'll be myself the harbinger and make joyful
> The hearing of my wife with your approach.
>
> (I. iv. 45–6)

'Harbinger' is cognate with 'harbour' and, like it, connotes safety and protection. In *Macbeth*, of course, safety is a leading theme. As Macbeth himself puts it, 'To be thus is nothing, / But to be safely thus' (III. i. 48–9). The witches introduce the theme of safe harbour in obscure seafaring riddles, where the first witch controls the winds and assigns them 'the very ports they blow' (I. iii. 15). She elaborately threatens sexual, psychological, and physical misfortune for Macbeth. The use of 'ports' here establishes an all-important connection between the witches and the Porter. Incidentally, those winds which create havoc in certain ports crop up again, connected with the birth motif, in Macbeth's soliloquy prior to Duncan's murder:

> pity, like a naked new-born babe
> Striding the blast, or heaven's cherubim hors'd
> Upon the sightless couriers of the air,
> Shall blow the horrid deed in every eye,
> That tears shall drown the wind.
>
> (I. vii. 21–5)[47]

Macbeth arrogantly invokes those very winds when he insists on seeing the witches' visions:

> answer me!
> Though you untie the winds and let them fight
> Against the churches; though the yesty waves
> Confound and swallow navigation up . . . .
>
> (IV. i. 51–4)

Oblivious of the consequences, Macbeth the sailor raises his own storm, thus fulfilling the witches' prophecy:

Though his bark cannot be lost,
Yet it shall be tempest-tost.

(I. iii. 24–5)

No safe port or harbour for Macbeth, then. In a final recognition of
the witches' trickery he says, 'be these juggling fiends no more
believ'd, / That palter with us in a double sense (v. viii. 19–20).
'Palter'– or *porter*? The witches are also porters. Their reports
transported Macbeth and his wife into the future prematurely.[48]
Ironically enough, Macduff, Macbeth's nemesis, was not borne for
his full time but delivered prematurely as well. The verb 'palter',
which means 'to mumble indistinctly' or 'to equivocate', is cognate
with the later German borrowing 'poltergeist', 'a noisy spirit'. And
the paltering of the witches is at one with the various other noises in
the play. Finally, what of the sound difference between 'palter' and
'porter'? We cannot conclusively claim that 'l' and 'r' were
assimilated before 't',[49] a phonological development which would
render the two words indistinguishable in pronunciation. We may
assume by analogy that 'palter' would have lost its 'l', since
Shakespeare rhymes 'halter'-'slaughter'-'after' in *King Lear*, [50] and
puns on *Walter/water* in *2 Henry VI*.[51] The loss of 'l' before 'd'
produces the rhyme 'chaudron'-'cauldron' in *Macbeth* (IV. i. 33–4).
A loss of 'l' and 'r' before 't' is indicated in the pun in *Lear* on *fault/
fart* at 'Do you smell a fault?' (I. i. 16). The evidence points to a
homophonic relationship between 'palter' and 'porter', thus decod-
ing perhaps the greatest of those 'palterings which yield their
meanings at unexpected times and places and which inspire an
ever-increasing vigilance as the play proceeds'.[52]

Perhaps the main support for my equation of 'palter' and 'porter'
may be drawn from the preceding line, where Macbeth mentions
'juggling fiends'. Juggling involves throwing things around, and an
attentive reading of *Macbeth* reveals a strong antithesis between
porting ('carrying') and throwing. Hence the wrestling imagery, as
when the Porter casts off 'his heavy burden of nocturnal drink'.[53]
Hence also the horrid images of Lady Macbeth, who at least implies
that she would rather throw her baby from her than give it maternal
support (I. vii. 54–9). Generally, the concept of throwing denotes
evil or is associated with evil characters in *Macbeth*. Cawdor is
'overthrown' (I. iii. 116) by treason and freely throws away his soul
(I. iv. 8–11). Macbeth would rather wear ('port') his golden
opinions than see them 'cast aside so soon' (I. vii. 34). The witches

throw poisoned ingredients into their cauldron (IV. i. 5). The Gentlewoman has watched a crazed Lady Macbeth 'throw her nightgown upon her' (v. i. 5–6). Like 'bear', 'throw' betokens retribution: 'Your leavy screens throw down' (v. vi. 1). And, again like its opposite number, 'bear', 'throw' occurs decisively before Macbeth's last fight: 'Before my body/I throw my warlike shield' (v. viii. 32–3). It is no wonder, then, that the agents of fate are characterised as 'juggling', for the word means 'throwing without letting drop'.[34] Juggling symbolises equivocation: throwing and bearing co-operate in an eternal dynamic. Thus the witches continually *port* the embryonic future through their malignant paltering.

The witches and Lady Macbeth are two examples of the 'evil mother' figure in Shakespeare, a folkloristic character type whose roots extend far back into his early work. Queen Margaret and Joan of Arc (*Henry VI*), [55] Tamora (*Titus Andronicus*), even the untamed Kate (*The Taming of the Shrew*) present figures which men subconsciously regard with deep anxiety and infantile fears embracing a whole complex of syndromes including suffocation, abandonment, and domination. These early characters establish the type, and are followed by comedic heroines such as Rosalind, Portia and Viola, in whom the *commedia dell'arte* convention of transsexual disguise externalises the masculine elements of evil motherhood. Having exhausted this comic tradition with the substituted spouse in *Twelfth Night*, Shakespeare confronts femininity entire in the problem plays. The heroines' sexual trickery (an extension of the disguise motif), coupled with men's inevitable need of women, prompt his almost immediate transition into tragedy. Here, masculine insecurity develops into a conflict illustrated by the ambiguous, enigmatic characterisation of Desdemona and Ophelia, and the contrasts between good and bad daughters in *King Lear*.

Throughout Shakespearian tragedy, negative associations obtain between women and the feminine element, water, and also between women and growth symbols. The pessimistic handling of arboreal imagery suggests a family tree warped, particularly throughout its feminine branches. Such references are frequently juxtaposed with liquid imagery. Ophelia falls off a tree and carries flowers downriver to her death; Desdemona, about to be strangled for an imaginary infidelity, sings of a willow-tree and carries a handkerchief whose strawberries have been interpreted as symbolising hymeneal blood;[56] Goneril is described as unnaturally slivering and dis-

branching from material sap (*King Lear*, iv. ii. 34–6); Lady
Macbeth, unable to wash the blood from her hands, does not live to
see Birnam Wood arrive. The whores in *Timon of Athens* roam a
forest where Timon vainly seeks roots for sustenance; and there is a
corn shortage in the Rome where Volumnia strives for dominance
over Coriolanus.

Cleopatra, associated with the fertile, muddy Nile, is not the last
of those unmanageable females who give Shakespeare's heroes so
much trouble; but her death crystallises an important penultimate
developmental stage of the 'evil mother' figure.[57] The picture of her
breastfeeding the fatal asp encourages comparison with nursing, a
parallel which she herself observes:

> Dost thou not see the baby at my breast,
> That sucks the nurse asleep?

> (*Antony and Cleopatra*, v. ii. 312–13)

With the passing of Cleopatra, turning maternal function in upon
herself, the 'evil mother' dies. The attendant insecurity which this
type produces in men expires with Coriolanus, the over-dependent
infant, 'boy of tears' (*Coriolanus*, v. vi. 101).

The infantile fear has been exorcised, along with the negative
creativity, warped woods and stagnant waters of the tragedies. The
evil mother revives in the romances, rising from the sea, bearing
flowers, now a regenerative daughter, chaste and pure, who
comforts her father and testifies to the honour of her mother in life's
evening-time.

5 'Beyond Beyond':
The Last Plays

With the last plays, we progress beyond pun, beyond figure, for these terms presuppose two realities: one expressed, the other reflected. The single reality in the romances is the survival of humanity through generation; and all verbal and visual imagery bends towards that theme. If the wordplay seems somehow thinner and the visual effects more extravagant than heretofore,[1] it is because Shakespeare is actualising his puns and verbal images, presenting them as stage realities conveying the theme of generation. Since familial continuity now provides the main dramatic action, generation metaphor becomes necessarily diluted: the very stage presence of families, family plots and stage imagery of fertility render it redundant. The concern in the last plays is with external rather than internal action. Now Shakespeare's verbal and visual images of generation do not merely express drama: they are one with it.

Families split asunder and reunite with the symbols of parturitive shipwreck and vegetative regrowth in the actional foreground. In the romances, 'the quality which formerly interpenetrated the story now is the story'.[2] Analysing *Pericles*, G. Wilson Knight pinpointed almost all the major images of the last plays, demonstrating their visual actualisation:

> what was formerly imagery becomes dramatic fact. The old image of storm gives us 'enter Pericles, wet'; that of bark-in-storm becomes a stage setting, with Pericles 'on shipboard'; the old association love = jewel is built into a personal sense of Thaisa's and Marina's jewel-like worth; the love-image of jewel-thrown-into-the-sea . . . becomes Thaisa in her jewel-stored coffin . . . thrown overboard. Shakespeare's continual reference to pagan deities works up to the 'feast of Neptune' and actual appearance of Diana. Finally, music, for so long a dramatic accompaniment

to scenes of love and reunion, becomes an active force in Cerimon's magic and explicitly mystical in Pericles' 'music of the spheres'. . . *Pericles* is the result of no sudden vision: it is Shakespeare's total poetry on the brink of self-knowledge.[3]

Literalisation of pregnancy in the problem plays had made possible for Shakespeare both tragic accommodation and the transcendence of romance. As opposed to earlier plays, where imagination creates or conceives shapes internally, the romances make manifest external creativity through the arts of design, mirroring human procreation. Shakespeare moves on to finer, purer images, masques and tableaux keyed to fertility with the subtlest cosmic reverberations. Jupiter and Juno descend to Posthumus with oracular promises of England's fertile future; Prospero (whose very name means 'growth')[4] arranges a masque of Iris, Ceres and Juno to sanctify Miranda's marriage; the coronation of Anne Boleyn, the vessel which will contain Elizabeth I, crosses the Globe stage in unparalleled panoply. Masque, which creates ideally visualised representations of society, is the greatest of those arts of tapestry which seek to duplicate Nature in the last plays.

Duplication, reduplication, immortality. Man's essential creativity, his ultimate victory over 'devouring Time', the bogeyman of the *Sonnets* (Sonnet xix, 1), consists in procreation, whereby his imprint on earth ensures immortality. In the *Sonnets*, Shakespeare had mentioned the importance of having children as insurance against oblivion. Two types of children predominated: actual children, who carry one's physical image beyond the grave, and brainchildren, the literary monuments which trumpet one's image to the world after death. Paulina affirms Perdita's resemblance to Leontes in an image which unites these two types:

> Behold, my lords,
> Although the print be little, the whole matter
> And copy of the father – eye, nose, lip.

> (*The Winter's Tale*, ii. iii. 97–9)

This image must have been close to Shakespeare's heart; maybe, in his final years, he contemplated his comforting best-loved daughter Susanna in similar terms. It recalls the image of Richard III as the 'right idea' of his father (*Richard III*, iii. vii. 13), the frequent man-as-book images in *Romeo and Juliet*, the book of Orsino's 'secret soul'

(*Twelfth Night*, I. iv. 14), Hamlet writing his thoughts on the table of his mind (*Hamlet*, I. v. 107). Those of Shakespeare's images which equate human continuity with imperishable literary achievement culminate in the picture of the new-born as the little reprint of her father.[5]

Here Shakespeare turned to dramatic use a trope which coloured the contemporary war of pamphlets between misogynists and philogynists.[6] Cornelius Agrippa compared woman to text in his exegetical vindication of femininity: 'Adam foundeth Erthe, but Eva is interpretate lyfe'.[7] The epoch see-sawed between attacks and apologies. Joseph Swetnam's notorious *Arraignment of Lewde, Idle, Froward, and Unconstant Women* (1615), a thinly-disguised attack on the whole sex, drew three females' refutations distinguished for their shimmering fury and crushing logic. 'Woman', wrote one defender of her sex in 1617, is 'the second Edition of the Epitome of the whole world, the second Tome of that goodly volume compiled by the great God of heaven and earth'.[8] Shakespeare had already characterised women in general as 'the books, the academes' (*Love's Labour's Lost*, IV. iii. 303), but in viewing the newborn child as a book he comes half-circle from the view in the *Sonnets*, where the printed work was seen as a child.[9]

Contrasted with the obscure 'Nature's hieroglyph' theme is Shakespeare's deliberate placing of the word 'pregnant' at key moments in the last plays. This provides support for the fertility plots and prepares the audience for the inevitable outcome. The final triumphal birth or regeneration does not occur *in vacuo* at each play's end: the fecund imagery of denouement echoes earlier focal dramatic points. Language of birth is used to foreshadow the conclusion, stating theme right at the pinnacle of the drama.

In *Pericles*, the rivalry between Marina and Philoten leads Dionyza to plot Marina's murder. The plan, revealed in Gower's Prologue to Act IV (ll. 43–6), has the unmistakable Shakespearian ring:

> cursed Dionyza hath
> The pregnant instrument of wrath present
> Prest for this blow. The unborn event
> I do commend to your content.

The murder never happens, since Marina is captured by bawds and placed in a situation which leads to familial rebirth, an 'unborn event' of which we hardly dream at this stage. In *Cymbeline*, Imogen finds Cloten's headless body, and, mistaking it for Posthumus's, cries, 'O, 'tis pregnant, pregnant!' (IV. ii. 325). Indeed so, since this discovery resolves part of the play and helps clear the way for final rebirths. The discovery of Perdita's identity in *The Winter's Tale* is reported thus:

> 2 GENTLEMAN.   . . . Has the King found his heir?
> 3 GENTLEMAN. Most true, if ever truth were pregnant by
> circumstance.
>
> (v. ii. 31–4)

In *The Tempest*, Sebastian compares Antonio's appearance to the posture of a woman in labour:

> The setting of thine eye and cheek proclaim
> A matter from thee; and a birth indeed
> Which throes thee much to yield.
>
> (II. i. 229–31)

The embryonic possibility giving Antonio such pregnant pause is Ferdinand's survival; Ferdinand does in fact survive the tempest to marry Miranda. Certainly, the language of pregnancy left its mark on criticism of the late plays: G. Wilson Knight uses the term 'impregnated' to describe dramatic effects throughout *The Crown of Life*, while Derek Traversi, in *Shakespeare: The Last Phase*, applauds the 'pregnant simplicity' of the romances.[10]

The procreative drift of the plays is suggested not only through their preparatory birth-language, but also through the fertile associations of three major images which Shakespeare equates with feminine excellence or the theme of birth: ships, flowers and gold. Like the image of woman-as-print, these comparisons also occur in the prose of anti- and pro-feminists in the Renaissance and early seventeenth century. Joseph Swetnam compares woman to the unprofitable bayleaf, and cautions that no more than gold is she to be superficially judged.[11] Barnabe Rich gives an extended metaphorical comparison between woman and ship, and acknowledges her to be made of the 'purified metall of man'.[12] Some years later, Elizabeth Joceline remarks that woman is like 'a well-ballanced ship that may beare all her saile'.[13] Just as Shakespeare introduced the pregnant poetic of his contemporaries into his early drama, so did he interweave these polemical images into his last plays, combining them all in the context of pregnancy and rebirth. The imagery of ships, flowers and gold, used singly and in combination, links the last plays together and puts Shakespeare's entire dramatic output in perspective.

Shakespeare had frequently associated ships, a common feminine symbol, with pregnancy and with women in general. Titania revelled in the comparison of her gravid votaress, 'swimming' along the strand, with the pregnant sails they had watched swell on the sea (*A Midsummer Night's Dream*, II. i. 128–34). Romeo derisively likened the Nurse in billowing skirts to 'A sail, a sail!' (*Romeo and Juliet*, II. iv. 108). The woman-as-ship image, linked to the ship-of-state archetype, characterises Margaret, wife of Henry VI (*3 Henry VI*, III. iii. 4–6). Angry with amorous Falstaff, Mrs Page vows, 'If he come under my hatches, I'll never to sea again' (*The Merry Wives of Windsor*, II. i. 95–6). In *Twelfth Night*, Act I scene ii, anticipating the shipwrecks of the romances, Viola appears after a shipwreck; Maria addresses her as a sailor (I. v. 215–18). We have already seen how Mariana's marital prospects aborted with the miscarriage of her brother Frederick in a 'perished vessel' (*Measure for Measure*, III. i. 216–23). Announcing Othello's marriage, Iago crudely tells Cassio, 'Faith, he to-night hath boarded a land carrack' (*Othello*, I. ii. 50). Enobarbus, recalling the picturesque Cleopatra seated in her royal barge, remembers among his details 'Purple the sails, and so perfumed that / The winds were love-sick with them' (*Antony and Cleopatra*, II. ii. 198–9). Eric Partridge offers salty definitions of 'board', 'board a land carrack', 'boarding', and 'boat hath a leak, her', but failed to spot any development between these vaginal jokes and the symbolism in the last plays, where the figure of the ship emerges triumphantly as a feminine metaphor. Shakespeare explicitly links ship-imagery with figurative pregnancy in the *Sonnets*, relating the feminine boat-symbol to his womblike, creative brain in a bitter comparison of his poetic abilities with his rival's:

> Was it the proud full sail of his great verse,
> Bound for the prize of all-too-precious you,
> That did my ripe thoughts in my brain inhearse,
> Making their tomb the womb wherein they grew?
>
> (Sonnet lxxxvi, 1–4)

Ship imagery is related to the feminine water-symbol, which had sorrowful implications in the tragedies. Macbeth had imagined the sea turning to blood (II. ii. 60–3), and Laertes's sad valedictory to Ophelia ran, 'Too much of water hast thou, poor Ophelia!' (*Hamlet*, IV. vii. 186); the 'poor soul' of gentle Desdemona's Willow Song sat weeping her cares and her life away into the stream at her feet (*Othello*, IV. iii. 41–8). Ophelia drowns; Marina, Perdita and Miranda rise from the sea. The female characters who heralded disaster in the tragedies are sources of new life in the romances. Images of shipwreck and tempest, while symbolising tragic shock and man's after accommodation,[14] also represent the parturitive split and cleavage of birth. This significance is explicit in the birth of Marina at sea, the coincidence between the discovery of Perdita and a storm, and the first appearance of Miranda after the tempest. In the last plays, water seems to represent the bath of life, and shipwreck the destruction of old corrupt values and receptive opening toward better standards and social rebirth. 'Birth' is understood either literally or as a metaphor for beneficial change in the world at large; *time*, etymologically linked with *tempest*,[15] is the womb, the 'wide gap' (*The Winter's Tale*, v. iii. 154) in which events germinate. Every moment is pregnant with the next.

Shakespeare juxtaposes verbal imagery of ships and birth at two key points in *Henry VIII*, indicating the play's thematic relationship with the romances preceding it. The first juxtaposition occurs with Henry's admitted failure to produce a masculine successor:[16]

> I weigh'd the danger which my realms stood in
> By this my issue's fail; and that gave to me
> Many a groaning throe. Thus hulling in
> Thè wild sea of my conscience, I did steer
> Towards this remedy . . . .

> (II. iv. 197–201)

This patriotic concern drives Henry into Anne's bed, and it is of further interest that the hopes of succession excited by Anne's coronation are suggested by the Third Gentleman's comparison of the proceedings to a tempest; pregnant women crane forward for the best view. Tempest and pregnancy unite with the creative arts of music and weaving as the crowd, a mysteriously interwoven sea of bodies, presses forward to see the new Queen, progenitress of Elizabeth I:

      such a noise arose
As the shrouds make at sea in a stiff tempest,
As loud and to as many tunes. Hats, cloaks, –
Doublets, I think, – flew up; and had their faces
Been loose, this day they had been lost. Such joy
I never saw before. Great belli'd women,
That had not half a week to go, like rams
In the old time of war, would shake the press
And make 'em reel before 'em. No man living
Could say "This is my wife" there; all were woven
So strangely in one piece.

                                (IV. i. 71–81)

After such an account, the end of the play comes as no surprise. This passage anticipates the ringing tones in which Cranmer ushers in the golden future promised by Elizabeth's birth.

Vegetation is pre-eminent among the other birth-symbols to which Shakespeare attaches more positive significance in his last plays. As we have already observed, the trees associated with the tragic heroines had negative connotations of stunted development, warped growth, or death. As in the case of the water-symbol, however, the tree image revives in the romances with an entirely opposite valuation. Vegetation forms part of the language of life, appearing in floral form in the hands of Marina and Perdita, and also in arboreal form, signifying a healthy, flourishing national development in *Cymbeline* and *Henry VIII*.

In the romances, vegetation gradually develops from a symbol of death to a symbol of life. Since flowers are associated with all the life-renewing heroines, one might plead for their acceptance as a life-symbol throughout, since even when flowers are mentioned in the context of grave-strewing, the idea of birth is never very far away. When decorating her mother's grave, Marina links her catalogue of flowers to the memory of her marine birth:

      No, I will rob Tellus of her weed,
      To strew thy green with flowers. The yellows, blues,
      The purple violets, and marigolds
      Shall as a carpet hang upon thy grave
      While summer-days doth last. Ay me! poor maid,
      Born in a tempest when my mother died,

This world to me is like a lasting storm,
Whirring me from my friends.

(*Pericles*, IV. i. 14–21)

Arviragus pledges himself to the constant sweetening of 'dead'
Fidele's grave with flowers 'while summer lasts' (*Cymbeline*, IV. ii.
218–24). Comatose Fidele/Imogen, reviving, thinks, 'These flowers
are like the pleasures of the world' (IV. ii. 296), an attitude similar to
Perdita's in *The Winter's Tale*, where flowers unequivocally represent love, life and laughter. Perdita yearns for Proserpina's spring
flowers to strew Florizel over

like a bank of love to lie and play on;
Not like a corse; or if, not to be buried,
But quick and in mine arms.

(IV. iv. 130–2)

The life-principle embodied in the Proserpina allusion actualises in
The Tempest with the onstage appearance of Ceres, who blesses the
marriage of Ferdinand and Miranda with fecundity:[17]

Earth's increase, foison plenty,
Barns and garners never empty,
Vines with clust'ring branches growing,
Plants with goodly burden bowing.
Spring come to you at the farthest
In the very end of harvest!
Scarcity and want shall shun you;
Ceres' blessing so is on you.

(IV. i. 110–17)

In *Henry VIII* the vines, corn, fields and agricultural plenty
associated with Ceres dominate Cranmer's prophetic vision of the
fertile future promised by Elizabeth's birth:

She shall be lov'd and fear'd; her own shall bless her;
Her foes shake like fields of beaten corn
And hang their heads with sorrow. Good grows with her.
In her days every man shall eat in safety

Under his own vine what he plants, and sing
The merry songs of peace to all his neighbours.

(v. v. 31–6)

Iterative tree imagery in *Pericles*, *Cymbeline* and *The Winter's Tale*
symbolises national and familial regeneration,[18] and the heavily
motivated agricultural imagery of *The Tempest* and *Henry VIII* has
been seen as weaving 'a myth of the national soul'.[19] With the burst
of fertility imagery surrounding Elizabeth's birth in *Henry VIII*,
Shakespeare crystallises the achievement of the age gone by as well
as his own genius. Cranmer finishes his speech with an arboreal
prophecy about the yet unborn James I, prefigured in the newborn
Elizabeth:

> CRANMER.   . . . he shall flourish
> And like a mountain cedar reach his branches
> To all the plains about him. Our children's children
> Shall see this, and bless Heaven.
> KING.   Thou speakest wonders.

(v. v. 53–6)

The 'wonder' associated with Shakespeare's romance heroines
inheres in their natural ability to better the human condition.
Indeed, the credibility of the female sex, so sadly lacking in the
tragedies, is triumphantly restored in the last plays by the inversion
of those very symbols which helped to create the tragic atmosphere
of distrust and panic. Vegetation (including trees and flowers) and
water (including ships and tempest), both linked in the tragedies
with death, revive in the romances as symbols of femininity and
birth. As early as *2 Henry VI*, Shakespeare juxtaposed these two
images in Suffolk's promise to Queen Margaret regarding the
elimination of her political enemies: 'one by one, we'll weed them
all at last, / And you yourself shall steer the happy helm' (i. iii. 103–
4). Weeds and ships – a strange mixed metaphor, apparently. But
the simultaneous application of vegetation and water images to
women culminates in the romances, with Florizel yearning for
Perdita, the flower-maiden, to be fixed in perpetual beauty of dance
like 'a wave o' th' sea' (*The Winter's Tale*, iv. iv. 140–3). Archetypal
associations with wood-nymphs and water-nymphs prevail, com-
parable to that natural sympathy between woman-woods and

woman-water in the myths of Daphne and Io, for instance.[20] Music, the regenerative and harmonising agent in the romance recognition scenes, is oddly associated with both flowers and sea in the 'Orpheus' song sung as a consolation to Queen Katherine of Aragon:

> Orpheus with his lute made trees
> And the mountain tops that freeze
>   Bow themselves when he did sing.
> To his music plants and flowers
> Ever sprung as sun and showers
>   There had made a lasting spring.
>
> Ever sprung as sun and showers
> Even the billows of the sea,
>   Hung their heads, and then lay by.
> In sweet music is such art,
> Killing care and grief of heart
>   Fall asleep, or hearing, die.
>
>   (*Henry VIII*, III. i. 3–14)

Katherine requests that her grave be strewn with 'maiden flowers' (IV. ii. 169) that the world may know her chastity. In *Pericles*, Marina, carrying maiden flowers to her mother's grave, is strangely reminded of her marine birth. The associations are concentrated, complex. Ships–flowers–music–birth. *The Two Noble Kinsmen*, whose right of inclusion in Shakespeare's canon has been convincingly urged on imagistic grounds,[21] opens with a prologue asserting the necessity of looking after Chaucer's 'baby', and then requesting the audience to prevent the ship (the drama) from sinking. Act I scene i reveals a wedding in the tradition of Shakespeare's romance masques, accompanied by a catalogue-of-spring-flowers fertility song. Here the ship image of the Prologue is applied to the brainchild, or the poetic product, while the flower imagery anticipates a fertile marriage between two humans. Either way, the feminine metaphor is friendly and benign, opening on new worlds and promising wonders.[22] Shakespeare's attitude toward women in the romances appears entirely at one with Ester Sowernam's inspiring reminder to her readers under misogynistic attack from Joseph Swetnam: 'You are women; in Creation, noble, in Redemption, gracious, in use most blessed; be not forgetfull of your selves, nor unthankefull to that Author from whom you receive all.'[23]

The third major image with which Shakespeare expresses feminine rarity is gold or jewels, to which he compares female pricelessness. Instead of portraying the worthless, fatal woman who, trapped by her biological and cultural role, wilfully or unconsciously betrays her husband/son/father, the romances shower with jewel-like radiance the feminine forces which subvert destruction and bigotry and create fertile environments. Anne Boleyn is especially interesting, and has not received enough critical attention in this regard. Shakespeare devotes an entire scene (II. iii) to informing the audience the price Henry is willing to pay for her proximity. The spiritual worth of the other romance heroines[24] actualises in the worldly honours which Henry heaps upon Anne, as detailed by the Chamberlain:

> That you may, fair lady,
> Perceive I speak sincerely, and high note's
> Ta'en of your many virtues, the King's Majesty
> Commends his good opinion of you, and
> Does purpose honour to you no less flowing
> Than Marchioness of Pembroke; to which title
> A thousand pound a year, annual support,
> Out of his grace he adds.

> (II. iii. 58-64)

The scene is crammed with bawdy language, playing particularly upon the *queen/quean* pun in discussing Anne's character and aspirations. This association supports Shakespeare's view of the romance heroines as queens, as royal creatures, in terms of both character and descent; the 'quean' stigma, ever-present in the tragedies (even Desdemona and Ophelia are seen as whores) gradually fades. Bawdy language is at last ennobled, since Shakespeare minimises Anne's marriage-breaking role to emphasise her worth, her value as potential mother for England's royal succession. Her rapid submission and acceptance of favours, despite her initial doubt and her sure awareness of Henry's sexual conditions, are seen as historical facts and patriotic glories. The Old Lady provides us with the dirty jokes, but any misgivings as to the purity of Anne's stretchable 'cheveril conscience' (II. iii. 32) dissolve in the sonority of the Chamberlain's cosmic estimate of her mettle:[25]

> I have perus'd her well.
> Beauty and honour in her are so mingled
> That they have caught the King; and who knows yet
> But from this lady may proceed a gem
> To lighten all this isle?

> (ii. iii. 75–9)

Like his association of ship and vegetation imagery with women, the connection between precious metals and birth had roots early in Shakespeare's work. This linkage derives in part from the semantics of the verb, 'coin', which uses money as the metaphor for the invention of an idea. In *Titus Andronicus*, Aaron gleefully contemplates how

> this gold must coin a stratagem,
> Which, cunningly effected, will beget
> A very excellent piece of villainy.

> (ii. iii. 5–7)

The Merchant of Venice deals with real and apparent feminine worth in terms of metals and uses the gold-birth association in Shylock's discussion with Antonio on loan and interest. Shylock offers a biblical parable about sheep-breeding and relates it to his own affairs:

> ANTONIO.   . . . is your gold and silver ewes and rams?
> SHYLOCK. I cannot tell; I make it breed as fast.

> (i. iii. 96–7)

Antonio, urging a purely business relationship between himself and Shylock, contemptuously says,

> If thou wilt lend this money, lend it not
> As to thy friends; for when did friendship take
> A breed for barren metal of his friend?

> (i. iii. 133–5)

Similar associations underlie the Clown's interchange with Viola in *Twelfth Night*. He has made her laugh; she has given him one coin.

CLOWN. Would not a pair of these have bred, sir?
VIOLA. Yes, being kept together and put to use.
CLOWN. I would play Lord Pandarus of Phrygia, sir, to bring a
Cressida to this Troilus.
VIOLA. I understand you, sir. 'Tis well begg'd.

(III. i. 55–60)

As we saw in *Othello*, the mental impregnation of Othello involves
the transfer of the purse of conceit from Iago to Othello.

Gold, the third major fertility symbol of Shakespeare's last plays,
was associated with both ships and flowers in his earlier dramatic
works. The plots of *The Comedy of Errors*, *The Merchant of Venice*,
and *Twelfth Night* connect gold with ships. For an association
of gold with vegetation, we need look no further than *Timon
of Athens*:

> Earth, yield me roots!
>
> (*Digging.*)
>
> Who seeks for better of thee, sauce his palate
> With thy most operant poison!
> What is here?
> Gold? Yellow, glittering, precious gold! No, gods,
> I am no idle votarist; roots, you clear heavens!

(IV. iii. 23–7)

The three images of gold, water, and vegetation uphold the
fertility theme of Shakespeare's last plays, and attach themselves in
particular to portrayal of the heroines. *The Two Noble Kinsmen*
provides instances of these symbols in total fusion and also relates
them to Shakespeare's pregnant creative endeavour as a whole.
Arcite's sylvan prayer to his absent guiding spirit, the fair Emilia,
provides ample evidence for not only Shakespeare's hand, but also
his heart, in the play:

> O Queen Emilia,
> Fresher than May, sweeter
> Than her gold buttons on the boughs, or all
> Th'enamelled knacks o' th' mead or garden, yea
> We challenge too the bank of any nymph

> That makes the stream seem flowers; thou, O jewel
> O' th' wood, o' th' world, hast likewise blest a place
> With thy sole presence.

(III. i. 4–11)

Here gold, water, flowers melt into a paean to womanhood.

The feminine metaphor in late Shakespeare represents the ultimate comfort and hope, as we see from Arcite's remarkable *consolatio in carcere* to his cousin Palamon. His daring birth images recall the fertile mental marriage and pregnant thought-processes of Richard II, immured at Pomfret:

> What worthy blessing
> Can be, but our imaginations
> May make it ours? And here being thus together
> We are an endless mine to one another;
> We are one another's wife, ever begetting
> New births of love; we are father, friends, acquaintance;
> We are in one another, families;
> I am your heir and you are mine; this place
> Is our inheritance: no hard oppressor
> Dare take this from us; here, with a little patience,
> We shall live long and loving.

(II. iii. 76–87)

Arcite's claim for the golden creativity of imagination, the 'endless mine', is the fundamental assumption upon which Shakespeare's dramatic work rests. Here all the sexual conflicts and androgynous exploits resolve. Harnessed to love, imagination is self-sufficient. Humans strive for the perfect union of their masculine and feminine elements to combat time and loneliness.

Just as Arcite reminds Palamon of his social obligation, so Shakespeare's Prologue to the play impresses upon the audience their responsibility to protect Chaucer's brainchild. The Shakespearian stamp is all the more obvious for the juxtaposition of birth and water imagery, entirely characteristic of the fertile, fluid romances, and the Prologue deserves lengthy citation, since no summary can hope to render its inherent Shakespearianness of both thought and image:

New plays and maidenheads are near akin,
Much follow'd both, for both much money gi'en,
If they stand sound and well: and a good play
Whose modest scenes blush on his marriage day
And shake to lose his honor – is like her
That after holy tie and first night's stir
Yet still is modesty, and still retains
More of the maid to sight, than husband's pains.
We pray our play may be so; for I am sure
It has a noble breeder and a pure,
A learned, and a poet never went
More famous yet 'twixt Po and silver Trent.
Chaucer, of all admir'd, the story gives,
There constant to eternity it lives;
If we let fall the nobleness of this,
And the first sound this child hear be a hiss,
How will it shake the bones of that good man
And make him cry from under ground . . . .

       it were an endless thing
And too ambitious, to aspire to him,
Weak as we are, and almost breathless swim
In this deep water. Do but you hold out
Your helping hands, and we shall tack about
And something do to save us . . . .

             (Prologue, 1–18, 22–7)

The colloquial tones, the rather coarse impact of the first two lines,
the rhyming couplets typify early seventeenth-century prologue
style. However, the feminine imagery, the view of the play as a
sinking baby, the direct correspondence urged between art and
human generative processes, and especially this appeal to the
audience to concern themselves with aesthetic nurture, all strongly
bespeak Shakespeare's work. In the Epilogue,[26] the comparison
between new plays and maidenheads reappears in the author's
challenge to 'he that has / Lov'd a young handsome wench' (ll. 5–6)
to come forth and damn the play, the implication being that anyone
who loves a virgin could not possibly pan this new, virginal play,
Chaucer's offspring.

    Shakespeare's propensity for feminine metaphor undoubtedly
encouraged some of the more exotic authorship theories which

identify him as various women.. Candidates for his laurels have
included Mary, Queen of Scots, Anne Hathaway, Anne Whately,
the Countess of Pembroke and the Countess of Rutland. George
McMichael and Edgar Glenn, reviewing these outlandish notions,
connect them with Shakespeare's feminine themes and imagery:

> A female Shakespeare is one way of explaining the uniquely
> feminine qualities some theorists have perceived in the works.
> Such qualities can be achieved, proponents of Shakespeare-as-
> female argue, only by one who was a woman, since men are not
> capable of understanding the complexities of the female mind.[27]

Such transsexual identification of great personalities works both
ways, however. There are those who would insist on Queen
Elizabeth I's masculinity, largely referrable to her political attitudes and achievements and her tenacious virginity. At least one
theorist proposes that Shakespeare and Elizabeth, the two greatest
personalities of the period, are identical, accounting the plays as the
'literary children' of Elizabeth's 'marriage to England'.[28] Writing
on Anne Whately's behalf in 1939, William Ross specifically
instanced the birth metaphor as proof of female authorship,
asserting that it is 'a metaphor which would not suggest itself to a
man, but which would not be strangely unnatural coming from
a woman'.[29]

As we have already noted, however, the many references to
pregnancy in connection with literary creativity in the works of
Shakespeare's contemporaries mark the generation metaphor as
one which did indeed suggest itself to a great many gentlemen, and
which enjoyed the status of a literary convention. The wide
receptivity to feminine metaphor is a manifestation of that matrism
which Gordon Rattray Taylor perceives as a sociological phenomenon in the English Renaissance. In *Sex in History*, Taylor
describes the effect of matrism upon Renaissance masculine
fashions:

> The suspicion that a somewhat matristic period was
> developing . . . receives confirmation from the clothing of the
> period, which underwent a rapid change from the time of Henry
> VIII to that of James I. In Henry's day, men's masculinity was
> emphasized by the short coat and tights. . . . In this reign it

would have been quite impossible to be in doubt about the sex of anyone even if seen only in silhouette. But by the end of the century men were wearing broad-skirted coats in rich materials, with lace collars, remarkably similar to the clothes worn by women; in looking at some of Mytens' portraits, one is unsure, for a moment, which sex is represented.[30]

Certainly, this androgynous fashion trend, which approximates to the 'unisex' of the present day, can be related to that literary taste which permitted Lyly to glory in the 'pregnant wit' of his Euphues.[31]

The tendency to relate the mechanism of pregnancy and birth to wit, creativity, aesthetic production and thought itself [32] perhaps reflects an improving status of women during the sixteenth century, but there still arises a perplexing dichotomy in those English sonnets which make of woman a dumb Petrarchan or Platonic icon (it really doesn't matter which) and obliquely praise the pregnant, fruitful striving of the masculine poet contemplating his two-dimensional idol. The woman is divested of her true femininity; the poet views her as a distant, austere object while appropriating her biological function to describe his own literary excellencies. This appreciation of woman as silent and motionless, however physically appealing, contrasts oddly with the poet's unfettered adoration of his own fertile mind. At the heart of a literary movement which allows true pregnancy – inventiveness, meaningfulness – to be solely masculine property, we detect a subtle misogyny. The troubadour poets contemplated their poems as the real object of their affection, rather than the woman celebrated; the Renaissance poets maintained this tradition.[33] Only instead of bestowing upon their artworks the language of love, heterosexual desire and *Frauendienst*,[34] they went one stage further, pouring into dedications and prologues for male patrons images of pregnancy. The metaphor of generation served as the vehicle wherein writers displayed the infant products of their fertile genius to the public. It became a thorough cliché in *belles lettres* during the sixteenth century, and already betrayed signs of debasement and decadence in the early years of the seventeenth in such florid pieces as Middleton's dedication to *The Ghost of Lucrece* (1600)[35] and Burre's dedication of Beaumont and Fletcher's *The Knight of the Burning Pestle* (1613) to Robert Keysar.[36] Mid-century and Restoration poets wrought the last perverse variations upon it, exemplified by Dryden's comparison of the virgin playwright to 'a mere Poetical Hermaphrodite'[37] and Cleveland's exhortation to his contemporaries

> Be dumb ye beggers of the rhiming trade,
> Geld your loose wits, and let your Muse be splaid.[38]

Whereas his fellow poets could see no further than their own pregnant inventiveness, Shakespeare envisaged his literary creations as fecund and generative as his own self. Nothing less than the primary image of life would express this view. Shakespeare widened the referential frame of the Renaissance pregnant poetic by working it into his dramatic plots, allowing fertility not only in himself, but also in his characters, male and female. In terms of the generation metaphor Shakespeare's broadest, most crucial themes are sounded: perception in the lyrical plays, thought and action in the problem plays and tragedies. It is because this metaphor carries universal appeal that his works evoke universal response. The use of this primary image ennobled the clichéd literary ideal of 'conceit', broadening it in the problem plays to encompass human conception, and ultimately tying actual and figurative generation together in a set of puns, verbal images and symbols which cannot be, and somehow should not be, fully explicable. The generation metaphor, at once familiar and unfathomable, makes the plays more accessible and more profound. Here is the ground of Shakespeare's lasting appeal: he speaks to us *originally*, in the language of human origin. There is no child in sight when Prospero blesses the force which breeds between Ferdinand and Miranda (*The Tempest*, iii. i. 75–6). Without love there is sterility, rotten branches, hopes drowned. With love, with imagination, Shakespeare brought forth for himself, his characters and his audience the new world which continually renews itself.

Appendix: Chronology of the Plays

The dates are approximate, and represent an adaptation of the information in Alfred Harbage, *Annals of English Drama, 975–1700*, 2nd edn, revised by Samuel Schoenbaum (Philadelphia, Penn.: University of Pennsylvania Press, 1964).

Year	Comedy	History	Problem play	Tragedy	Romance
1591		2H6			
		3H6			
1592	Errors	1H6			
1593	Two Gents	R3			
1594	Shrew			Titus	
1595	LLL*	R2*		Romeo*	
	Dream*				
1596	Merchant V.	John			
1597		1H4			
		2H4			
1598	Much Ado				
1599	AYLI	H5		Julius	
1600	Wiv.				
	Twelfth N.				
1601			Hamlet†		
1602			All's Well		
			Troilus		
1603					
1604			Measure		
				Othello	
1605				Lear	
1606				Macbeth	
1607				Antony	
				Timon	
1608				Coriolanus	Pericles
1609					Cymbeline
1610					Wint.
1611					Temp.
1612					
1613		H8			Kinsmen

* I have classed these four dramas as lyrical plays.

† I have classed *Hamlet* as a problem play in the present study because of its position in Shakespeare's canon before *All's Well*, *Troilus* and *Measure for Measure*, although it is normally regarded as a tragedy.

Notes

1. Timothy Bright, *A Treatise of Melancholy* (London, 1586) p. 45.
2. See, for example, Barnabe Barnes, *A Divine Centurie of Spirituall Sonnets* (London, 1595) Sonnet lxxx, 1–2: 'A blast of winde, a momentarie breath, / A watrie bubble symbolizde with ayre.'
3. The myth of Athene's birth illustrates the double meaning of 'conception' and symbolises the birth of thought. For a similar account in Christian tradition, see John 1 : 1–14, particularly verses 1, 4 and 14: 'In the beginning was the Worde, and the Worde was with God and the Worde was God. . . . In it was life, and the life was the light of men. . . . And the Worde was made flesh.' Biblical citations refer to *The Geneva Bible* (1560; facsimile repr. Madison: University of Wisconsin Press, 1969), since that is the version that Shakespeare is most likely to have read.
4. See *Popol Vuh*, Sylvanus Morley and Delia Goetz, trs. (Norman: University of Oklahoma Press, 1956). This sacred book of the ancient Quiché Maya relates how the deities Tepeu (male) and Gucumatz (female) come together and think hard overnight, 'then while they meditated, it became clear to them that when dawn would break, man must appear' (p. 82).
5. Genesis 3:7, 4:1.
6. Francis Bacon, *Of the Proficiencie and Advancement of Learning, Divine and Humane* (1605) sig. G4r.
7. The English Renaissance redefined literary aims and methods in more inward terms than the Greeks, who insisted upon the imitative qualities of art. See Maurice W. Bundy, ' "Invention" and "Imagination" in the Renaissance', *JEGP*, xxix (1930) 535–45.
8. Stephen Hawes, *The Pastime of Pleasure* (1517) ed. William Edward Mead, Early English Text Society, vol. clxxviii (London: Oxford University Press, 1928) ll. 708–11.
9. Sir Philip Sidney, *The Defence of Poesie* (1595) sig. B4v–C1v.
10. Roger Ascham, *The Scholemaster* (1570) ed. Edward Arber (London: n.p., 1870) pp. 32–4.
11. Gertrude Jobes, *Dictionary of Mythology, Folklore, and Symbols* (New York: Scarecrow Press, 1962) vol. i, p. 559. Compare Robert Briffault, *The Mothers* (1927), abridged, and with an introduction by Gordon Rattray Taylor (1959; repr. New York: Grosset and Dunlap, 1963) p. 101: 'In the earliest Egyptian hieroglyphs the pot is the symbol of womanhood. . . . In Greece, the pot was an emblem of fecundity.'
12. For a discussion of contemporary medical theories, see Walter Pagel, 'Medieval and Renaissance Contributions to Knowledge of the Brain and Its

Functions', in *The History and Philosophy of Knowledge of the Brain and Its Functions* (1965; repr. Amsterdam: B. M. Israel, 1973) pp. 95–114. See also Bundy, in *JEGP*, xxix, 537, regarding the importance of mediaeval psychology in the Renaissance.

13. Henry Ansgar Kelly, *The Matrimonial Trials of Henry VIII* (Stanford, Calif.: Stanford University Press, 1976), writes of Henry, 'His virtual childlessness . . . and especially his failure to produce a male heir, must have had frightening implications for him, who was only the second king in a new royal line. This dynastic crisis, which really lasted throughout his reign, must never be lost sight of as a powerful reason for his discontent with unfruitful unions and his desire to enter into more promising marriages' (pp. 32–3).

14. See Richard Foster Jones, *The Triumph of the English Language: A Survey of Opinions Concerning the Vernacular from the Introduction of Printing to the Restoration* (Stanford, Calif.: Stanford University Press, 1952) p. 189.

15. Samuel Daniel, *Musophilus*, ll. 969–74, in *The Complete Works in Verse and Prose of Samuel Daniel*, ed. Alexander B. Grosart (1885; repr. New York: Russell and Russell, 1963) vol. 1, p. 256.

16. Thomas Raynalde, *The Byrth of Mankynde, otherwyse named The Womans Booke* (1560), was the third edition of his revision in 1545 of Richard Jonas's *The Byrth of Mankynde Newly Translated out of Laten into Englyshe* (1540). The 'Laten', *De partu hominis*, was itself a translation of Eucharius Roeslin's *Der swangern Frauwen und Hebammen Rosegarten* (1513), an obstetrical book which appeared in numerous editions and was translated into several languages throughout the sixteenth century. Raynalde's revision of Jonas includes a significant amount of pro-feminist polemic, reflected by his addition of 'The Womans Booke' to the title, and his political prologue directed toward women in general as opposed to Jonas's complimentary prologue to Queen Katherine Howard. The Raynalde revision saw approximately one dozen editions between 1545 and 1655, with a new edition appearing almost every decade; the Jonas was not reprinted. All citations in the text refer to Raynalde's edition of 1560. Sig. C2v–C3r.

17. Gershon Legman's term. See the section on 'Male Motherhood of Authorship' in his *Rationale of the Dirty Joke: An Analysis of Sexual Humor* (New York: Grove Press, 1968) pp. 592–6.

18. Compare the expression *corpus*, used since the early eighteenth century to denote a writer's total production, and the classification (since late eighteenth and early nineteenth century) of literature by *genres* (literally, 'families').

19. See Milton's *Areopagitica*, in *Milton's Prose*, ed. Malcolm W. Wallace (1925; repr. London: Oxford University Press, 1959) p. 280: 'As good almost kill a Man, as kill a good Book', and compare Pope, *The Dunciad* (1742) I, 121–2, in *The Poems of Alexander Pope*, ed. John Butt (1963; repr. London: Methuen, 1965), on the unproductive Colley Cibber: 'Round him much Embryo, much Abortion lay, / Much future Ode, and abdicated Play.' In *The Man Who Loved Women* (1977), Truffaut's male doctor opines to a gonorrheal patient and would-be author, 'To create a book and have it published is as wonderful as giving birth to a child.'

20. Sir Philip Sidney, *Astrophel and Stella* (1591) sig. B1r.

21. George Chapman, *Achilles Shield* (1598) sig. D2r.

22. George Turberville, *Epitaphes, Epigrams, Songs and Sonets* (1567) sig.* 5ʳ.
23. George Whetstone, *The Rocke of Regard* (1576) sig.¶ 2ʳ.
24. Sir Philip Sidney, *The Countess of Pembrokes Arcadia* (1590) sig. A3.
25. Edmund Spenser, *The Shepheardes Calender* (1579) sig.¶ 1ᵛ.
26. Christopher Marlowe, *Hero and Leander* (1598) sig. A3ʳ.
27. In *An Anthology of Elizabethan Dedications and Prefaces*, ed. Clara Gebert (Philadelphia: University of Pennsylvania Press, 1963) p. 163.
28. Ibid., p. 251.
29. In *The Dramatic Works of Thomas Dekker*, ed. Fredson Bowers (Cambridge: Cambridge University Press, 1962) vol. II, pp. 497–8.
30. In *An Anthology of Elizabethan Dedications*, p. 112.
31. Ibid., pp. 80–1.
32. John Lyly, *Euphues and his England*, 2nd edn (1606) sig. A2ᵛ. Legman is alive to the implications of latent homosexuality in this syndrome. I reproduce in part a revealing and hilarious modern example which he gives as 'the most total statement of the whole idea' (*Rationale of the Dirty Joke*, p. 593), drawn from K[urt] M. S[tein], *Gemixte Pickles* (Chicago, 1927), written in comic Anglo-German: 'Bei den Quantitäts von neuen Books zu judgeh wo daily geadvertised werden, sollt man denken es iss a dernsight easier a Brainchild zu haben denn a neun pount Baby. In a way iss dass so, aber net entirely. . . in dieser Line haben die Ladies plenty competition. Das andere Bissness haben sie pretty solid bei'm tail [!] und aufgesewed, but an Gehirnkindern haben sie noch kein exclusive Patent. . . . Notmitstanding und in shpite davon, iss es oft painvoll sowohl als dangerous der selfcontainteh Parent even von a ganz kleinen, slimmen, Volume zu sein. . . .' Legman concludes (p. 596), '*I would suggest as axiomatic that: the masochist element in male motherhood is invariably best displayed where the woman figure is also present, as father*. . . . Where the motherhood is strictly monosexual . . . the emphasis is of course straight anti-woman and homosexual.' It is interesting to find the fashionable bisexuality of Renaissance authors manifesting itself in female metaphor. At the same time, we must remember that the choice of metaphors for creativity is limited, and the metaphor of generation is to some extent an inevitable choice. My axiomatic suggestion, as opposed to Legman's, would be that the choice of a birth image is understandable, perhaps unavoidable. Where we find lurid and overblown comparisons extending the metaphor beyond reasonable aesthetic limits, we may at least suspect bisexuality. Where this metaphor is coupled with covert or stated insult to women, the emphasis is probably latent homosexual.
33. In *An Anthology of Elizabethan Dedications*, pp. 155–6.
34. In *Elizabethan Critical Essays*, ed. G. Gregory Smith (1904; repr. London: Oxford University Press, 1950) vol. I, p. 194.
35. Edmund Spenser, *The Shepheardes Calender* (1579) sig.¶ 3ʳ.
36. Gabriel Harvey, *Pierce's Supererogation* (1593), in *Elizabethan Critical Essays*, vol. II, pp. 249–50.
37. Ibid., p. 259.
38. Gabriel Harvey, *Foure Letters* (1592) p. 235.
39. Gabriel Harvey, *Pierce's Supererogation* (1593) p. 269.
40. Ibid., p. 277.
41. Thomas Nashe, Epistle Dedicatorie to *Have With You to Saffron-Walden* (1596)

in *The Works of Thomas Nashe*, ed. Ronald B. McKerrow (Oxford: Basil Blackwell, 1958) vol. III, p. 11.

42. Nashe's *Commendation of Sidney*, prefacing *Astrophel and Stella* (1591), in *Elizabethan Critical Essays*, vol. II, p. 227.

43. Raynalde, *Birth of Mankynde*, sig. B3^v.

44. Ibid., sig. B4^v–B5^r.

45. Alexander Barclay, *The Eclogues of Alexander Barclay from the Original Edition by John Cawood* (1570) ed. Beatrice White, Early English Text Society, vol. CLXXV (London: Oxford University Press, 1928) Prologue, ll. 1–4.

46. Thomas Wilson, *The Arte of Rhetorique* (1553) sig. P2^v.

47. *Zepheria* (1594) sig. A4^r.

48. See *The Winter's Tale*, III. ii. 83–5, where Leontes tells Hermione, 'Your actions are my dreams; / You had a bastard by Polixenes, / And I but dream'd it.'

49. Marjorie Garber, *Dream in Shakespeare: From Metaphor to Metamorphosis* (New Haven, Conn.: Yale University Press, 1974).

50. Derek Traversi, *Shakespeare: The Last Phase* (1955; repr. Stanford, Calif.: Stanford University Press, 1969) p. 3.

51. Henri Fluchère, *Shakespeare and the Elizabethans* (1947), trs. Guy Hamilton (New York: Hill and Wang, 1956) p. 162.

52. See Garber on dream, and compare Kirby Farrell, *Shakespeare's Creation: The Language of Magic and Play* (Amherst: University of Massachusetts Press, 1975).

53. Ben Jonson also urged a family resemblance between the plays and Shakespeare in his eulogy 'To the Memory of My Beloved, the Authour Mr. William Shakespeare: And What He Hath Left Us': 'Looke how the fathers face / Lives in his issue, even so, the race / Of Shakespeare's minde, and manners brightly shines / In his well torned, and true filed lines.'

CHAPTER 2

1. See, for example, James L. Calderwood, 'Shakespeare's Evolving Imagery: *2 Henry VI*', *ES*, XLVIII (1967) 481–93.

2. Herbert McArthur, 'Romeo's Loquacious Friend', *SQ*, x (1959) 35–44. Sydney Thomas, 'The Queen Mab Speech in *Romeo and Juliet*', *ShS*, xxv (1972) 73–80, believes that the speech was not originally in the play, that it is entirely a 'display aria' (p. 80), with the exception of the last three lines. Garber, *Dream in Shakespeare* (p. 37), highlights the theme of self-deception, and Barbara Everett, '*Romeo and Juliet*: The Nurse's Story', *CritQ*, XIV (1972) 129–39, focuses on the storytelling (p. 139).

3. I agree with Garber's observation that 'the "law of association" is the organizing principle of his wit; puns and riddles, his weapons and signs' (*Dream in Shakespeare*, p. 35), and follow her three-part division of the Mab speech (pp. 40–2).

4. Jobes, *Dictionary of Mythology*, vol. II, p. 1082.

5. *Larousse Encyclopaedia of Mythology* (New York: Prometheus Press, 1960) p. 247.

6. Jobes, *Dictionary of Mythology*, vol. II, p. 1031.

7. Compare Mercutio's complaint at II. iv. 99–100: 'Thou desir'st me to stop in my tale against the hair' – where the sense is clear by association. See Eric Partridge, *Shakespeare's Bawdy*, 2nd edn (New York: E. P. Dutton, 1969), for other references.

8. Compare the horse/woman correspondence in Henry's seduction of young Kate of France (*Henry V*, v. ii. 141–8). Lear, in misogynistic mood, rails on the whole sex: 'Down from the waist they are Centaurs, / Though women all above' (*King Lear*, iv. vi. 126–7). This correspondence has a background in mythology and legend: see Jobes, *Dictionary of Mythology*, vol. i, pp. 789–92 for the folkloric association between Horsel (the Swabian love-goddess) and hostelry.

9. Ibid., p. 710.

10. For the characteristics of nightmare, see Rossell Hope Robbins, *The Encyclopaedia of Witchcraft and Demonology* (London: Peter Nevill, 1959) pp. 340–1, 356. According to Robbins, the mare (derived from Old English *mare*, 'demon', not *mere*, 'horse') sits on the chest and causes feelings of suffocation. Old French *cauchemar* ('nightmare') means 'trample-demon'. The mare also attacked horses. Of nightmare Robbins observes, 'in the Hebrew Zohar it was said that a man's erotic dreams are caused by a succubus lying with him to bear evil spirits' (p. 356). Robbins also quotes T. Bond, *An Essay on the Incubus or Nightmare* (1763): 'The nightmare generally seizes people lying on their backs.'

11. McArthur (in *SQ*, x, 44) places the onset of Romeo's tragic awareness in his next speech. This is just a little late: Romeo enters adulthood with his interruption of Mercutio.

12. See the Nurse's reminiscence at i. iii. 16–48 about Juliet's weaning. The Friar's worldview is expressed entirely in breastfeeding images after the balcony scene between Romeo and Juliet (ii. ii). This imagery tragically recalls to us the discrepancy between the youth of Romeo and Juliet and the depth of their experience, while bolstering the hidden theme that we are all children on Mother Earth (ii. iii. 9–12).

13. Garber felicitously calls the Queen Mab speech the 'fledgling doctrine of creative dream' (*Dream in Shakespeare*, p. 42).

14. Partridge, *Shakespeare's Bawdy*, pp. 47–8.

15. The linkage of dream and birth is typical of Shakespeare. In *Much Ado About Nothing*, even the verb 'dream' calls up the pregnant association, as when the Friar describes the consequences of the plot which he has dreamed up: 'not for that dream I on this strange course, / But on this travail look for greater birth' (iv. i. 214–15).

16. For the idea of a pregnant autumn, compare Sonnet xcvii, 6–8, where Shakespeare describes autumn after the death of summer: 'The teeming autumn, big with rich increase, / Bearing the wanton burden of the prime, / Like widowed wombs after their lords' decease.'

17. Ships, a common feminine symbol, are fully discussed in Chapter 5 below.

18. R. W. Dent, 'Imagination in *A Midsummer Night's Dream*', *SQ*, xv (1964) 115–29 (p. 119).

19. Thomas Vicary, *The Anatomie of the Bodie of Man* (1548; repr. 1577) ed. Frederick J. Furnivall and Percy Furnivall (London: N. Trübner, 1888). Vicary was Sergeant Chirurgion to Henry VIII, Edward VI, Mary I and Elizabeth I, and served at St Bartholomew's Hospital. He writes, 'in the wane of the Moone, the brayne discendeth downwardes, and vanisheth in substaunce of vertue: for then the Brayne shrinketh togeather in it selfe, and is not so fully obedient to the spirit of feeling'. Vicary notes that effects on

'lunatike' or epileptic individuals are most severe in the first and last quarters (p. 33).

20. Fredric Cook, *Acting: Being Natural. Professional Artist Letter* (Los Angeles: Los Angeles Academy of Dramatic Art) 17 Feb 1977.

21. Anca Vlasopoulos, 'The Ritual of Midsummer: A Pattern for *A Midsummer Night's Dream*', *RenQ*, XXXI (1978) no. 2, 21–9 (p. 26).

22. Irving Oyle, *Time, Space and the Mind* (Millbrae, Calif.: Celestial Arts, 1976) pp. 128, 125, 127. The fragility of this peace was brilliantly hinted at in the 1978 San Diego production of *A Midsummer Night's Dream*, where, owing to a final directorial touch, Titania and Oberon appeared to be quarrelling again immediately after the stage bows.

23. See John Erskine Hankins, *Shakespeare's Derived Imagery* (Lawrence: University of Kansas Press, 1953) pp. 97–8.

24. Jerome Mandel, 'Dream and Imagination in Shakespeare', *SQ*, XXIV (1973) 61–8 (p. 65): 'Dreams stand in the same relation to the play-world as the play-world stands in relation to the real world.'

25. See Edwin Clarke and Kenneth Dewhurst, *An Illustrated History of Brain Function* (Oxford: Sanford Publications, 1972) pp. 40–1.

26. Ralph Berry, *Shakespeare's Comedies: Explorations in Form* (Princeton, N. J.: Princeton University Press, 1972) pp. 9–10.

27. Oberon's striking metonymy of IV. i. 56–9: 'And that same dew which sometime on the buds / Was wont to swell like round and orient pearls, / Stood now within the pretty flowerets' eyes / Like tears that did their own disgrace bewail.'

28. In *Venus and Adonis*, Venus's creation through tears exhibits certain similarities with Queen Isabel's. Perhaps Shakespeare recalled Venus's perspective glass when he came to write *Richard II*:

> Upon his hurt she looks so steadfastly
> That her sight dazzling makes the wound seem three;
> And then she reprehends her mangling eye,
> That makes more gashes where no breach should be.
> His face seems twain, each several limb is doubled;
> For oft the eye mistakes, the brain being troubled.
>
> 'My tongue cannot express my grief for one,
> And yet,' quoth she, 'behold two Adons dead! . . .'
>
> (ll. 1063–70)

This image was turned to comic use in *A Midsummer Night's Dream*, in Hermia's words on double vision: 'Methinks I see these things with parted eye, / When everything seems double' (IV. i. 193–4).

29. Eric La Guardia, 'Ceremony and History: The Problem of Symbol from *Richard II* to *Henry V*', in *Pacific Coast Studies in Shakespeare*, ed. Waldo McNeir and Thelma N. Greenfield (Eugene: University of Oregon Books, 1966) pp. 68–88 (p. 77).

30. Ibid., p. 78.

31. The 'plant–Plantagenet' correspondence causes the confusion: Shakespeare conflates images of heredity with images of vegetative growth. Not until *Macbeth* does he fully master this particular image cluster.

32. I owe the adjective 'symphonic' to Richard D. Altick, 'Symphonic Imagery in *Richard II*', *PMLA*, LXII (1947) 339–65.
33. La Guardia's comparison (in *Pacific Coast Studies*, p. 77) of Theseus's 'airy nothing' with Isabel's 'nothing' is injudicious, since Theseus's speech assumes that an object exists which the imagination mistakes for something else. Isabel, on the other hand, cannot name her fear because there is nothing at all to be seen. She does not miscreate; she creates.
34. S. K. Heninger, Jr, oversimplified Isabel's role in 'The Sun-King Analogy in *Richard II*', *SQ*, XI (1960) 319–27, calling her a 'lovely Queen . . . who devotedly mourns her lord in idealized terms of eulogy' (p. 321). Such sentimentalisation risks obscuring Isabel's considerable significance.
35. See Traversi, *Shakespeare: The Last Phase*, p. 5, for possibly the most short-sighted critique ever written on Richard's metaphor of conception: 'This is not great verse. . . . It is important chiefly as an exercise in the writing of balanced and corrected blank verse, an exercise which helped to ensure that, when the great flood of associated ideas and sensations which characterise Shakespeare's mature poetry came to demand expression, his verse forms should not break down into incoherence under the strain.'
36. Paul A. Jorgensen, 'Much Ado About *Nothing*,' in *Redeeming Shakespeare's Words* (Berkeley, Calif.: University of California Press, 1962) pp. 22–42 (p. 37). Rightly insisting on the analogy between aesthetic and divine creation, Jorgensen interprets the dramatic tension between *nothing* and *something* in Shakespeare as reflecting the dramatist's own generative process.
37. 'Richard is', says Wylie Sypher in *Four Stages of Renaissance Style: Transformations in Art and Literature 1400–1700* (New York: Doubleday, 1955) p. 93, '. . . merely a contour of royalty, who studies his worn image in the mirror he holds before him, telling, in his solemn tremolo, sad stories of the death of kings, playing the wanton with his woes, descending lithely to his little, little grave'.
38. Jorgensen, in *Redeeming Shakespeare's Words*, p. 38.
39. See Chapter 4 below for a discussion of *conceptio per aurem* – the aural impregnation theme.
40. Just what *Love's Labour's Lost* does mean has excited a good deal of thematic and stylistic criticism in recent years. See J. J. Anderson, 'The Morality of *Love's Labour's Lost*', *ShS*, XXIV (1971) 55–62; Trevor Lennam, ' "The Ventricle of Memory": Wit and Wisdom in *Love's Labour's Lost*', *SQ*, XXIV (1973) 54–61; Catherine M. McLay, 'The Dialogues of Spring and Winter: A Key to the Unity of *Love's Labour's Lost*', *SQ*, XVIII (1967) 119–28; Terence Hawkes, 'Shakespeare's Talking Animals,' *ShS*, XXIV (1971) 47–54; and Joseph Westlund, 'Fancy and Achievement in *Love's Labour's Lost*', *SQ*, XVIII (1967) 37–46.
41. Herbert Ellis, *Shakespeare's Lusty Punning in 'Love's Labour's Lost'* (The Hague and Paris: Mouton, 1973) p. 104. See his entire discussion of *wit*, pp. 103–10. He does not cite the marvellous Don Pedro speech to Benedick in *Much Ado About Nothing* (v. i. 160–5): 'I'll tell thee how Beatrice prais'd thy wit the other day. I said thou hadst a fine wit. "True," said she, "a fine little one." "No," said I, "a great wit." "Right," says she, "a great gross one." "Nay," said I, "a good wit." "Just," said she, "it hurts nobody" ' (with a pun on *nobody/no body*!)
42. Vicary's description of the *pia mater* membrane merits full quotation: 'next

unto this pannicle there is another pannicle called *Pia mater*, or meeke mother, because it is so softe and tender unto the brayne. Of whose creation it is to be noted as of Duramater, for the original of their fyrst creation is of one kind, both from the Hart and the Lyver, and is mother of the very substance of the brayne. Why it is called Pia mater, is, for because it is so softe and tender over the brayne, that it nourisheth the brayne and feedeth it, as doth a loving mother unto her tender childe or babe; for it is not so tough and harde as is Duramater. . . . this Pannicle doth circumvolve or lappe al the substaunce of the brayne' (*Anatomie*, pp. 29–30). For the incorporation of these words into mediaeval medical terminology, see Ynez Violé O'Neill, 'William of Conches and the Cerebral Membranes', *Clio Medica*, II (1967) 13–21.

43. Ellis does not include 'capable' in his glossary. Partridge gives the meanings 'sexually capable; nubile' (*Shakespeare's Bawdy*, p. 76).

44. As so often in Shakespeare, a linguistic idea progresses toward actual plot function in the later plays. Here Rosaline discusses the possibility of a joke's prosperity – will it take seed in the listener's mind? In *Measure for Measure*, the Duke outlines his plot to Isabella, who anticipates its success in these lines: 'I trust it will grow to a most prosperous perfection' (III. i. 271–2). Edmund ends his soliloquy about illegitimate birth with 'I grow; I prosper. / Now, gods, stand up for bastards!' (*King Lear*, I. ii. 21–2). In *The Tempest*, a character named Prospero controls the action. For the shift from abstract to concrete, or rather the move from linguistic to dramatic idea-portrayal, see Chapter 5 on the romances.

45. Partridge, *Shakespeare's Bawdy*, pp. 21–2.

CHAPTER 3

1. E. M. W. Tillyard, *Shakespeare's Problem Plays* (London: Chatto & Windus, 1960) p. 1.

2. William Witherle Lawrence, *Shakespeare's Problem Comedies*, 2nd edn (New York: Frederick Ungar, 1960) p. 20.

3. See the *pregn-* root entries in John Florio, *Queen Anna's New World of Words, or Dictionarie of the Italian and English Tongues, Collected, and Newly Much Augmented* (London, 1611; originally published in 1598 as *Worlde of Wordes*).

4. In *The Songs and Sonets of John Donne*, ed. Theodore Redpath (1956; repr. London: Methuen, 1967) p. 88.

5. Robert Cawdrey, *A Table Alphabeticall . . .* (1604) ed. Robert A. Peters (Gainesville, Fla.: Scholars' Facsimiles and Reprints, 1966).

6. See the excellent article by John E. Hankins, 'Hamlet's "God Kissing Carrion": A Theory of the Generation of Life', *PMLA*, LXIV (1949) 507–16, and the reply by Evan K. Gibson, ' "Conception is a blessing" ', ibid., pp. 1236–8.

7. A pun already used by Shakespeare in *Love's Labour's Lost* (v. ii. 169–71):

> MOTH. . . . with your sun-beamed eyes –
> BOYET. They will not answer to that epithet;
> You were best call it 'daughter-beamed eyes'.

8. Compare Gertrude's description of Hamlet as a brooding dove in the graveyard.scene, v. i. 307–11:

> This is mere madness,
> And thus a while the fit will work on him.
> Anon, as patient as the female dove
> When that her golden couplets are disclos'd,
> His silence will sit drooping.

9. Compare Claudius's incredibly stubborn knees at the moment of prayer, III. iii. 70–1: 'Bow, stubborn knees, and heart with strings of steel, / Be soft as sinews of the new-born babe!' This is one of the very many language and imagery links between Hamlet and Claudius in the play.

10. See, for example, Harry Morris, '*Hamlet* as a *Memento Mori* Poem', *PMLA*, LXXXV (1970) 1035–40.

11. See S. F. Johnson, 'The Regeneration of Hamlet', *SQ*, III (1952) 187–207; and Peter G. Phialas, 'Hamlet and the Grave-Maker', *JEGP*, LXIII (1964) 226–34.

12. Wolfgang H. Clemen, *The Development of Shakespeare's Imagery* (1952; repr. London: Methuen, 1969) p. 106.

13. Caroline F. E. Spurgeon, *Shakespeare's Imagery and What It Tells Us* (1935; repr. Cambridge: Cambridge University Press, 1968) pp. 173–4.

14. See T. McAlindon, 'Language, Style and Meaning in *Troilus and Cressida*', *PMLA*, LXXXIV (1969) 29–43. In his note 2 on p. 29, McAlindon compares the abortiveness of *Troilus and Cressida* to that of *Love's Labour's Lost* in terms of their inkhorn vocabulary, noticing a discrepancy between 'words and deeds, words and character, words and situation' in both plays. I submit that it is the image of failed pregnancy which overwhelmingly suggests and, in fact, makes plain, this discrepancy. Both plays set out to conceive, both plays end in abortion.

15. See Michael Shapiro, ' "The Web of our Life": Human Frailty and Mutual Redemption in *All's Well That Ends Well*', *JEGP*, LXXI (1972) 514–26, for the theory that Helena's pregnancy, 'the living proof of her marriage bond', prefigures the redemptive filial love of the last plays.

16. Parolles is openly hostile to marriage, seeing the housewife as a negative drain upon the man's vital juices: 'He wears his honour in a box unseen, / That hugs his kicky-wicky here at home, / Spending his manly marrow in her arms, / Which should sustain the bound and high curvet / Of Mars's fiery steed' (II. iii. 296–300). Jay L. Halio, '*All's Well That Ends Well*', *SQ*, xv (1964) 33–43, interprets the play in terms of the rivalry between Helena and Parolles for Bertram's love, contrasting Parolles's hollow sterility, manifested in his great drum, with Helena's pregnant womb, teeming with the 'rich burden of life' (p. 42).

17. Lavatch extends the pun later, describing himself as 'a fool . . . at a woman's service, and a knave at a man's' (IV. iv. 25–6).

18. See John F. Adams, '*All's Well That Ends Well*: The Pardox of Procreation', *SQ*, XII (1961) 261–71.

19. Garber, *Dream in Shakespeare*, p. 15.

20. See Michel Grivelet, ' "And Measure Still for Measure": sur quelques études récentes de la pièce de Shakespeare', *EA*, XXI (1968) 65–72; and Jonathan R. Price, '*Measure for Measure* and the Critics: Towards a New Approach', *SQ*, xx (1969) 178–204, for excellent surveys of the criticism on *Measure for Measure*.

Both Grivelet and Price see the need for new blood in criticism of this play.

21. See Clifford Leech, 'The "Meaning" of *Measure for Measure*', *ShS*, III (1950) 55–73. Leech calls attention to the irony of Juliet's name: it is the same as Romeo's Juliet. Maybe Shakespeare was shooting down some of his own sacred cows in these middle years.

22. James S. Trombetta, 'Versions of Dying in *Measure for Measure*', *ELR*, VI (1976) 60–76 (p. 66).

23. For an ingenious treatment of other paradoxical assumptions behind *Measure for Measure*, see Wylie Sypher, 'Shakespeare as Casuist: *Measure for Measure*', *SR*, LVIII (1950) 262–80.

24. James Black, 'The Unfolding of *Measure for Measure*', *ShS*, XXVI (1972) 119–28, oversimplifies: 'As Angelo has put the letter of the old law into effect, so Mariana sets the letter of forgiveness and love in act. This she does through the bed-trick' (p. 124). It is the *Duke* who conceives the plan, quite transparently putting Mariana up to it, as my quotation from the play makes clear.

25. The city–woman correspondence has, of course, biblical precedents: consider, for example, the descriptions of Jerusalem as harlot. And, as for the implications of the fountain, the Catholic liturgy refers to Mary as *fons pietatis*. There is a certain amount of sexual symbolism inherent in giving someone the keys to a city, cutting the ribbons before the gates, and so on. In *Measure for Measure*, there are other 'feminine' locations beside the city itself – notably the garden, with its inner walls and passages and little key (IV. i. 28–36). A rendezvous is planned there 'upon the heavy middle of the night' (IV. i. 35). Trombetta calls the prison 'not tomb but womb' (in *ELR*, VI. 63), pointing to the simultaneity of Claudio's intended execution and Juliet's delivery.

26. For the dirty possibilities inherent in 'will', see Shakespeare's Sonnets CXXXV and CXXXVI. Beyond the meanings 'determination' and 'sexual organ', there often lies the third punning level of Shakespeare's name.

27. The term is analogous to Partridge's 'puden-synomy', *Shakespeare's Bawdy*, pp. 21–2.

28. See Joanne Altieri, 'Style and Social Disorder in *Measure for Measure*', *SQ*, XXV (1974) 6–16 (p. 16), for a description of *Measure for Measure*'s setting as non-green and urban, qualities which contrast strikingly with Shakespeare's earlier comic settings.

29. See the arguments in M. R. Ridley, *On Reading Shakespeare* (London: Humphrey Milford, 1940).

30. J. V. Cunningham, 'Woe or Wonder: The Emotional Effect of Shakespearian Tragedy', in *Tradition and Poetic Structure* (Denver, Col.: Alan Swallow, 1960) p. 21: 'the experience of each reader is different, and different at each separate reading, and . . . some of these experiences . . . are quite far removed from others'.

31. See, for example, Roy W. Battenhouse, '*Measure for Measure* and the Christian Doctrine of Atonement', *PMLA*, LXI (1946) 1029–59; and Wilbur D. Dunkel, 'Law and Equity in *Measure for Measure*', *SQ*, XIII (1962) 275–85, and note 20 above.

32. Morris Henry Partee, 'The Comic Unity of *Measure for Measure*', *Genre*, VI (1973) 274–93 (p. 278).

33. Lawrence W. Hyman, 'The Unity of *Measure for Measure*', *MLQ*, XXXVI (1975) 3–20 (p. 9).

34. Hilda M. Hulme, *Explorations in Shakespeare's Language: Some Problems of Lexical Meaning in the Dramatic Text* (Aberdeen: Longman Green, 1962) p. 94.

CHAPTER 4

1. William Flint Thrall and Addison Hibbard, *A Handbook to Literature* (1936), revised and enlarged by C. Hugh Holman (New York: Odyssey Press, 1960) p. 32.
2. Spurgeon, *Shakespeare's Imagery*, p. 5.
3. Brian Vickers, *The Artistry of Shakespeare's Prose* (London: Methuen, 1968) p. 20.
4. Robert Bechtold Heilman, *This Great Stage: Image and Structure in King Lear* (1948; repr. Seattle: University of Washington Press, 1963) p. 9. Heilman is describing the effect on the reader of recurrent words and their reverberations throughout Shakespearian tragedy.
5. See, for example, James Kirsch, *Shakespeare's Royal Self* (New York: G. P. Putnam's Sons, for the C. G. Jung Foundation for Analytical Psychology, 1966).
6. See Theodore Spencer, *Shakespeare and the Nature of Man* (New York: Macmillan, 1942) p. 153, on the distinctive 'worlds' of Shakespeare's tragedies.
7. See Hulme, *Explorations*, pp. 14–15.
8. Alexander Welsh, 'The Loss of Men and Getting of Children: *All's Well That Ends Well* and *Measure for Measure*', *MLR*, LXXIII (1978) 17–28 (pp. 24–5).
9. *Timon of Athens*, I. i. 92. This quotation was used as an article title by Inga Stina-Ewbank, ' "More Pregnantly than Words": Some Uses and Limitations of Visual Symbolism', *ShS*, XXIV (1971) 13–18.
10. Kirsch, *Shakespeare's Royal Self*, p. 239.
11. See Robert B. Heilman, *Magic in the Web* (Lexington: University of Kentucky Press, 1956). Heilman notes Iago's evident predilection for birth-imagery, and feels that he generally uses such images in the context of revelation. It does seem obvious, however, that these images also denote creativity, particularly since Iago uses them in the process of aesthetic or empirical invention, i.e. when creating art or telling lies. The play's images of birth are 'used almost exclusively in connection with wrongdoing. In the play of love itself there is almost no note of the renewal of life; fertility belongs to evil' (p. 100). This paradox is characteristic of Shakespeare's mature tragedies.
12. I cannot agree with Barbara Heliodora C. De Mendonça's observation in '*Othello*: A Tragedy Built on Comic Structure', *ShS*, XXI (1968) 31–8, that Iago's 'fertile [!!] but shallow imagination does not carry him beyond the simple desire to demoralize Othello' (p. 33). For a superior analysis of the comic values underlying the play, see Susan Snyder, '*Othello* and the Conventions of Romantic Comedy', *RenD*, V (1972) 123–41.
13. *Elizabethan Critical Essays*, vol. II, p. 3.
14. Clemen, *Development of Shakespeare's Imagery*, p. 122.
15. Vicary, *Anatomie*, p. 77.
16. Othello's 'pain' in the forehead is generally taken to be a reference to the cuckold's horns. The reading I propose may perhaps suggest some new staging for the scene.

17. Robert H. Rogers, 'Endopsychic Drama in *Othello*', *SQ*, xx (1969) 205–16, calls for 'a satisfactory account . . . of the precise psychosexual relationship between Othello and Iago if the pregnant suggestion that they are doubles is to be accepted' (p. 209). In Rogers's description of the suggestion – 'pregnant' – lies his answer, of course, although I believe that he used this particular epithet unconsciously, tending, like many Shakespearian critics, to use birth-imagery in Shakespearian interpretation. For a similarly unconscious bullseye hit, compare Barbara Everett, 'Reflections on the Sentimentalist's *Othello*', *CritQ*, III (1961) 127–39, who speculates on the outcome 'if this primal energy [Othello's] can be "*married*", as it were, to a desire to destroy and corrupt, implanted by Iago' (p. 131, emphasis added).

18. Paul A. Jorgensen, ' "Perplex'd in the Extreme": The Role of Thought in *Othello*', *SQ*, xv (1964) 265–75 (p. 265).

19. *Paradise Lost*, ix, 733–8, in *Poetical Works of John Milton*, ed. Helen Darbishire (Oxford: Clarendon Press, 1962) vol. I, pp. 200–1 (emphasis added). See William B. Hunter, Jr, 'Eve's Demonic Dream', *ELH*, xiii (1946) 255–65, for some seventeenth-century views of Eve's dream. His citations reveal how prevalent the language of pregnancy was in accounts of satanically induced dreams.

20. For a thorough account of the motif in mediaeval Annunciation representations, and the antitheses between Eve and Mary, see Gertrud Schiller, *Iconography of Christian Art*, vol. I (1966), trs. Janet Seligman (Greenwich, Conn.: New York Graphic Society, 1971) pp. 40–6.

21. Edmund Spenser, 'An Hymne of Heavenly Love', in *Fowre Hymnes* (1596) sig. D3^r.

22. Ibid., sig. D4^r.

23. David Greene, 'Exploring Music – Something of a Mystery', *Musical Heritage Review*, II, no. 16 (18 Dec 1978) p. 47, gives an interesting example of Renaissance imitation of God: apparently the writing of musical suites in sets of six was intended to parallel the Deity's six-day creation of Earth. Renaissance artists were seeking to duplicate the processes described in Genesis.

24. See M. M. Mahood, *Shakespeare's Wordplay* (London: Methuen, 1957) p. 28: 'Shakespeare's puns have an active dramatic function which is very much the critic's concern. They may be "in character" or they may be a vital part of the play's thought.'

25. The 'mother' was a type of melancholy related to hysteria and ascribed chiefly to women since its source was supposed to be the womb. See Kenneth Muir's note on these lines in the New Arden edition of *King Lear* (1964; repr. London, Methuen, 1969) p. 85.

26. William R. Elton, *King Lear and the Gods* (San Marino, Calif.: The Huntington Library, 1966) pp. 120–1. Cf. the Heilman passage cited in note 11 above.

27. Compare Cordelia's parting shot to her sisters: 'Well may you prosper!' (I. i. 285).

28. Clemen, *Development of Shakespeare's Imagery*, p. 135.

29. See Robert H. West, 'Sex and Pessimism in *King Lear*', *SQ*, xi (1960) 55–60: Lear's 'sex horror grounds in his sense of tainted generation' (p. 58). Thomas Raynalde addresses the same question of sex hatred in the Prologue to his *Byrth of Mankynde* (1560), reasoning that if woman's genitals were truly abhorrent, then surgeons would shun their wives: 'I knowe nothyng in woman so privie ne

so secrete, that they shoulde nede to care who knewe of it, neyther is there any part in woman more to be abhorred, than in man. And yf the knowledge of suche thinges whiche commonly be called the womans privities, shoulde diminishe the hartie love and estimation of a woman in the minde of man, then by this reason, Phisitians and Chyrurgians wyves should greatly be abhorred misbeloved of theyr husbandes. And I myselfe lykewyse, whiche wryteth this booke, shoulde mervaylously above many other abhorre or lothe women' (sig. B7ᵛ–B8ʳ).

30. In *The Well-Wrought Urn: Studies in the Structure of Poetry* (New York: Harcourt, Brace, 1947) pp. 21–46.

31. For perhaps the most outraged response to Cleanth Brooks's interpretation, see Elmer Edgar Stoll, 'Symbolism in Shakespeare', *MLR*, XLII (1947) 9–23. In his scathing rebuttal of Brooks, Stoll scorns symbolic criticism, confessing huffily, 'In all my life I have never read, or even much endeavoured to read, a cipher or a riddle' (p. 10). Such narrow-mindedness leads inevitably to his conclusions (pp. 11–12): 'If, moreover, *Macbeth* should turn out after all to be a symbolical drama, it would of course be a startling, prodigious exception. I know of none in Shakespeare or the whole Elizabethan theatre. Of anything like our modern symbolism – meaning the thing said and also suggesting another . . . there is in Shakespeare . . . scarcely any trace. The three apparitions . . . are but effigies or emblems . . . with no hidden significance.' Stoll's cultural deprivation is also apparent in his stinging thrust on paradox (p. 12): 'And paradox, of which Mr. Brooks seems enamoured and obsessed, if there is any appreciable element of it in Shakespeare's dramatic art, whether in the action or the rhetoric, it has quite escaped me. . . . In dramatic character or situation the paradoxical hardly appears, except in Milton's Satan, before the Romantic movement.' For an equally irrational attack on symbolical or motific interpretations, cf. W. R. Keast, 'Imagery and Meaning in the Interpretation of *Lear*', *MP*, XLIV (1947) 225–37, where his note 18 (p. 63) attacks Robert B. Heilman at the lowest critical level: 'Mr Heilman, with his leisure to trace evanescent coincidences of words, his note cards, his opportunity to extract every last drop of ambiguity from a line.'

32. Brooks, *The Well-Wrought Urn*, p. 43.

33. Caroline Spurgeon, *Shakespeare's Imagery*, p. 326, supposed that the image of ill-fitting clothes suggested Macbeth's spiritual pettiness, citing the images as representing 'a small ignoble man encumbered and degraded by garments unsuited to him'. Brooks carefully points out (*The Well-Wrought Urn*, p. 32) that Macbeth's discomfort stems from the fact that the clothes he wears are *stolen* rather than too big.

34. Ibid., p. 44.

35. See III. v. 10–13: 'all you have done/Hath been but for a wayward son, / Spiteful and wrathful; who as others do, / Loves for his own ends, not for you.'

36. A favourite theme for misogynists, who never tire of emphasising Lady Macbeth's fiendishness. See, for example, D. W. Harding, 'Women's Fantasy of Manhood: A Shakespearian Theme', *SQ*, XX (1969) 245–53. For a defence of Lady Macbeth (a very rare occurrence), see Bill Goode, 'How Little the Lady Knew Her Lord: A Note on *Macbeth*', *AI*, XX (1963) 349–86. Goode theorises that Lady Macbeth underestimated her husband's ambition: he could not contemplate murder, but could effect it, whereas she could

contemplate it but not do the deed. Lady Macbeth's disintegration starts early on and Macbeth grows more and more independent of her, keeping her mystified and disturbed.

37. See Dennis Biggins, 'Sexuality, Witchcraft, and Violence in *Macbeth*', *ShakS*, VIII (1975) 255–78. Biggins draws parallels between the witches and Lady Macbeth and Macbeth's relationships with both, referring on p. 263 to the witches' 'demonic bisexuality'.

38. Cf. Mahood, *Shakespeare's Wordplay*, p. 135: 'Macbeth has no children but acts of violence against others.' We recall also Macduff's anguished scream at the news of his family's murder by Macbeth: 'He has no children' (IV. iii. 216).

39. See John B. Harcourt, 'I Pray You, Remember the Porter', *SQ*, XII (1961) 393–402.

40. Michael J. B. Allen, 'Macbeth's Genial Porter', *ELR*, IV (1974) 326–36. Passages cited: pp. 327, 331, 329, 327.

41. Raynalde, *Birth of Mankynde*, sig. D1^r. These terms also appear in Jonas's translation (1540).

42. See Allen, in *ELR*, IV, 329: 'The porter keeps the "portal" . . . the porter also "ports".'

43. Cf. the liturgical 'Qui tollis peccata mundi', which suggests the *tolerability* of sins. I assume a relationship between *tollere* and *tolerare*.

44. A technique first recognised by E. A. Armstrong in *Shakespeare's Imagination* (London: Lindsay Drummond, 1946) p. 84ff. Armstrong explains Shakespeare's frequent, apparently illogical juxtaposition of 'turkey' and 'pistol' by way of their common missing link, 'cock'.

45. Brooks writes (*The Well-Wrought Urn*, p. 33): 'The metaphor may seem hopelessly mixed, and a full and accurate analysis of such mixed metaphors in terms of the premises of Shakespeare's style waits upon some critic who will have to consider not only this passage but many more like it in Shakespeare.'

46. I quote verbatim from the *OED*'s entry at *harbinger*.'

47. Brooks (*The Well-Wrought Urn*, pp. 37–8) found the combination of 'babe' and 'striding the blast' incongruous. However, beyond the ingenious explanation Brooks provides, Shakespeare recapitulates this motif in the important discussion between Malcolm and Macduff in Act IV scene iii. Macduff, the retributive baby of the play, urges, 'Let us . . . *Bestride* our down-fall'n birthdom' (IV. iii. 3, emphasis added)'. The babe does after all stride the blast unleashed by Macbeth.

48. The letter which transports Lady Macbeth into the future concludes with the words, 'This have I thought good to deliver thee' (I. v. 11), bolstering the birth theme yet again.

49. See Helge Kökeritz, *Shakespeare's Pronunciation*, 2nd edn (New Haven, Conn.: Yale University Press, 1960) p. 310, and also p. 315: there is 'a good deal of evidence' that 'r' was silent before other consonants. Cf. E. J. Dobson, *English Pronunciation 1500–1700* (Oxford: Clarendon Press, 1957) vol. II, p. 967, which mentions Bullokar's loss of 'r' before 't' in 'hurt'. Regarding 'l', Dobson confirms (pp. 988–9) an absorption of 'l' before consonant by a preceding vowel (in the case of Middle English 'au' or 'ou'). He insists, however, that a loss of 'l' before 't' was 'not normal' in Standard English. Conversely, Kökeritz maintains (p. 183) that the retention of 'l' before 't' indicated pedantry.

50. Kökeritz cites this example (p. 183).

51. Suffolk identifies the name 'Walter' with the prophesied means of his death: 'By water I should die' (IV. i. 35) and suggests to Walter Whitmore an alternate pronunciation: 'Thy name is Gualtier, being rightly sounded' (IV. i. 37) to allay his bloody-mindedness.

52. Allen, in *ELR*, IV, 336.

53. Ibid., p. 330.

54. The *OED*'s definitions at *juggle*, in all its forms, mention trickery in a general sense only. But see also W. W. Skeat, *Etymological Dictionary of the English Language*, 4th edn (Oxford: Clarendon Press, 1974), which defines 'juggler' as 'one who employs sleight of hand'. The more contemporary reading I offer is based on our understanding of the word today, although circus tradition and Shakespeare's own thought behind the line would seem to suggest the idea of 'balancing' in this context.

55. See David M. Bevington, 'The Domineering Female in *1 Henry VI*', *ShakS*, II (1967) 51–8.

56. Lynda E. Boose, 'Othello's Handkerchief: 'The Recognizance and Pledge of Love'' ', *ELR*, V (1975) 360–74.

57. Recent years have seen a spate of articles dealing with the 'evil mother' figure in late Shakespearian tragedy. See David B. Barron, '*Coriolanus*: Portrait of the Artist as Infant', *AI*, XIX (1962) 171–93, which analyses the dependence of Coriolanus on his mother, highlighting the correspondence between Rome, the mother-city, and Volumnia, the mother actual. Coriolanus's standpoint *vis-à-vis* both is encapsulated in his assertion 'My birthplace hate I' (IV. iv. 23). Barron pursues similar lines of approach in 'The Babe That Milks: An Organic Study of *Macbeth*', *AI*, XVII (1960) 133–51, theorising that Macbeth submits to the female principle by putting his fate in the hands of women.

CHAPTER 5

1. Clemen, *Development of Shakespeare's Imagery*, pp. 179–80.

2. G. Wilson Knight, *The Crown of Life: Essays in Interpretation of Shakespeare's Final Plays* (1947; repr. New York: Barnes and Noble, 1966) p. 37.

3. Ibid., pp. 72–3.

4. See note 44 to Chapter 2 above.

5. The modern science replication of life through DNA uses the same life-as-book imagery: the basic chemical of life, DNA, is 'transcribed' in order to recreate life through RNA. RNA is then 'translated' into protein and life is duplicated. DNA itself is identified by the cracking of a genetic code which biologists call 'the genetic alphabet'. Compare also the language of behavioural science, which talks of the 'scripting' and 'imprinting' of human personality. An interesting semantic development occurs in the case of the word 'text', cognate with Latin *testa*, 'saucepan', used as slang for 'head' in Roman Gaul. *Tête* and 'text' – head and book – have cognate Romance roots.

6. See the sources cited in Celeste Turner Wright's articles, 'The Amazons in Elizabethan Literature', *SP*, XXXVII (1940) 433–56; 'Something More About Eve', *SP*, XLI (1944) 156–68; and 'The Elizabethan Female Worthies', *SP*, XLIII (1946) 629–43.

7. Cornelius Agrippa von Nettesheim, *The Commendation of Matrimony* . . . , trs. David Clapam (London, 1522?), sig. A3^r.

8. Constantia Munda, *The Worming of a Mad Dogge: or, a Soppe for Cerberus the Jaylor of Hell. No Confutation but a Sharpe Redargution of the Bayter of Women* (London, 1617) sig. B2^r.

9. Compare Ben Jonson's view of his son as his 'best piece of poetrie'.

10. Knight on the tragedies: 'the phraseology is intensely impregnated with moral and theological concepts', and 'the scene is impregnated with a grimness of intention' (*Crown of Life*, pp. 38, 39); on *The Winter's Tale*: Perdita's poetry 'is strongly impregnated with fertility suggestion' (p. 106); on *Henry VIII*: 'Can a Christian mythology be impregnated with the necessary dramatic force without sacrilege or bathos?' (p. 257). See especially Knight's remarks on the romances, which he believes to be 'impregnated with a far higher order of dramatic belief' (p. 204). Compare Traversi, who discusses the 'pregnant simplicity' (*Shakespeare: The Last Phase*, p. 42) of the denouement in *Pericles* and marvels at the Shepherd's 'simple, pregnant observation' (p. 136) at the centre of *The Winter's Tale*. See note 17 to Chapter 4 above.

11. Joseph Swetnam, *The Araignment of Lewde, Idle, Froward, and Unconstant Women: Or the Vanitie of Them, Choose You Whether. With a Commendacion of Wise, Vertuous and Honest Women* . . . (London, 1617) sig. E4^v.

12. Barnabe Rich, *The Excellency of Good Women. The Honour and Estimation that Belongeth unto Them. The Infallible Markes Whereby to Know Them* (London, 1613) sig. B3^r–C1^r, A4^r.

13. Elizabeth Jocelin, *The Mothers Legacie, To Her Unborne Childe* (London, 1624) sig. B6^r.

14. Knight, *Crown of Life*, p. 36ff.

15. See Linda Fitz, 'The Vocabulary of The Tempest' (Dissertation, University of California at Los Angeles, 1970) p. 193, on the etymology of 'tempest' from Latin *tempus*. On its relationship to the themes of time and rebirth, see her Chapter 8, pp. 188–211: 'The Vocabulary of Hope and Regeneration'.

16. On the Renaissance belief in the genetic superiority of males, and the desirability of having masculine children, see Jürgen Schäfer, 'When They Marry, They Get Wenches', *SQ*, XXII (1971) 203–11.

17. Clemen, *The Development of Shakespeare's Imagery*, p. 179, observes, 'Hardly in any other passage has Shakespeare ever concentrated so much sensuous exuberance and pregnant wealth of imagery as in the verses exchanged between Ceres and Iris.' Cf. note 10 above, and also note 17 to Chapter 4.

18. See James O. Wood, 'The Running Image in *Pericles*', *ShakS*, v (1969) 248–52; William B. Thorne, '*Cymbeline*: "Lopp'd Branches" and the Concept of Regeneration', *SQ*, XXIX (1969) 143–59; and William O. Scott, 'Seasons and Flowers in *The Winter's Tale*', *SQ*, XIV (1963) 411–17.

19. Knight, *Crown of Life*, p. 255.

20. The *Larousse Encyclopaedia of Mythology* (New York: Prometheus Press, 1960) mentions the *rusalka*, a female Slavonic mythological figure associated with both woods and water (pp. 302–3). She apparently represented the spirit of a drowned maiden and enjoyed a double existence, 'aquatic and sylvan' (p. 302), hiding in the water during the winter until the warm spring waters could no longer support a spirit of death, at which time she flew into the trees,

abode of the dead. Compare Ophelia as negative, and the romance heroines as positive, sides of this archetype.

21. Marco Mincoff, 'The Authorship of *The Two Noble Kinsmen*', *ES*, XXXIII (1952) 97–115, deals with a great many images, but does not press his case sufficiently far. The Shakespearian overtones in the play warrant further study. See Paul Bertram, *Shakespeare and The Two Noble Kinsmen* (New Brunswick, N. J.: Rutgers University Press, 1965), for a view that Shakespeare is solely responsible for the play.

22. See Linda Fitz, 'The Vocabulary of the Tempest', on the overtones of 'wonder' in *The Tempest* and its semantic and thematic relationship to the name 'Miranda'.

23. Ester Sowernam, *Ester Hath Hang'd Haman: or An Answere to a Lewd Pamphlet, entituled, The Arraignment of Women. With the Arraignment of Lewd, Idle, Froward, and Unconstant Men, and Husbands* . . . (London, 1617), sig. A3ʳ. Cf. note 8 above.

24. Traversi and Knight both noted the jewel or gold imagery in Shakespeare's representation of Thaisa, Marina, Imogen and Perdita.

25. Note that Regan travesties the precious-metal image in her smug self-comparison with Goneril: 'I am made of that self metal as my sister, / And prize me at her worth' (*King Lear*, I. i. 71–2).

26. The Epilogue is rather inferior to the Prologue. The fact that it is crammed with 'ye's leads one to suspect Fletcherian authorship.

27. *Shakespeare and His Rivals: A Casebook on the Authorship Controversy*, ed. George McMichael and Edgar M. Glenn (New York: Odyssey Press, 1962) p. 145.

28. George Elliot Sweet, *Shake-speare: The Mystery* (Stanford, Calif.: Stanford University Press, 1956) p. 83.

29. William Ross, *The Story of Anne Whately and William Shaxpere* (Glasgow: W. and R. Holmes, 1939) p. 13, writing on Sonnet lxxxvi, quoted in *Shakespeare and His Rivals*, p. 141.

30. Gordon Rattray Taylor, *Sex in History* (1953; repr. London: Harper and Row, 1973) p. 149.

31. John Lyly, *Euphues. The Anatomy of Wyt* . . . (London, 1578) sig. B2ʳ: 'hys pregnaunt wytte'. Compare Lyly's comment on Philautus, Euphues's friend: 'Whether his pregnant wit, or his pleasant conceits wrought the greater liking in the minde of Euphues I know not for certeyntie' (sig. B4ᵛ).

32. See Taylor, *Sex in History*, pp. 135–6, on the tendency of matrist societies to assimilate female figures to Wisdom or Divine Knowledge, etc., in contrast with 'the patrist symbol of a male deity representing authority'. He mentions that 'the Gnostics had worshipped divine wisdom under the name Sophia . . . and the Cathars similarly worshipped the Virgin as Our Lady Of Thought'.

33. Edward I. Condren, 'The Troubadour and His Labor of Love', *Mediaeval Studies*, XXXIV (1972) 174–95.

34. Ibid., p. 195.

35. Thomas Middleton, *The Ghost of Lucrece* (1600) ed. Joseph Quincy Adams (facsimile repr. New York: Charles Scribner's Sons, 1937), sig. A2ʳ, the dedication to Lord Compton, to whom Middleton wishes 'the fruit of eternal fruition'. He hails him as 'patron to the child-house of my vayne', 'Godfather to th' issue of my brain', and 'Baptizer of mine infant lines'.

36. Burre speaks of the play as a child sent into the world, whose indifference almost killed it, and begs Keysar's patronage. He likens himself to a foster-father, Keysar to a nurse, Beaumont and Fletcher to a father, and the play to a child, and closes in the fervent hope that the father will beget a younger brother to the present brainchild. The whole dedication is a remarkable illustration of the themes and images discussed in Chapter 1 above.

37. In *The Prologues and Epilogues of John Dryden: A Critical Edition*, ed. William Bradford Gardner (New York: Columbia University Press, 1951), piece lxiv, l. 35, pp. 107–8, entitled simply 'Prologue'. Lines 1–8 are as spectacular as the reader could wish:

> Gallants, a bashful Poet bids me say
> He's come to lose his Maidenhead to day,
> Be not too fierce, for he's but green of *Age*;
> And ne're, till now, debauch'd upon the Stage.
> He wants the suff'ring part of Resolution;
> And comes with blushes to his Execution.
> E'er you deflow'r his Muse, he hopes the Pit
> Will make some settlement upon his Wit.

38. 'The Hecatomb to his Mistresse', ll. 1–2, in *The Poems of John Cleveland*, ed. Brian Morris and Eleanor Wittington (Oxford: Clarendon Press, 1967) p. 50.

Select Bibliography

PRIMARY SOURCES

Agrippa, Cornelius von Nettesheim, *The Commendation of Matrimony* . . . , trs. David Clapam (London, n.d. [1522?]).

Ascham, Roger, *The Scholemaster*, ed. Edward Arber (London: n.p., 1870).

Bacon, Francis, *Of the Proficiencie and Advancement of Learning, Divine and Humane* (London: n.p., 1605).

Barclay, Alexander, *The Eclogues of Alexander Barclay from the Original Edition by John Cawood*, ed. Beatrice White, Early English Text Society, vol. CLXXV (London: Oxford University Press, 1928).

Barnes, Barnabe, *A Divine Centurie of Spirituall Sonnets* (London, 1586).

Beaumont, Francis, and Fletcher, John, *The Knight of the Burning Pestle* (London, 1613).

The Bible and Holy Scriptures Conteyned in the Olde and Newe Testament (The Geneva Bible) (1560; facsimile repr. Madison: University of Wisconsin Press, 1969).

Bright, Timothy, *A Treatise of Melancholy* (London, 1586).

Cawdrey, Robert, *A Table Alphabeticall* (London, 1604).

Chapman, George, *Achilles Shield* (London, 1598).

Cleveland, John, *The Poems of John Cleveland*, ed. Brian Morris and Eleanor Wittington (Oxford: Clarendon Press, 1967).

Daniel, Samuel, *The Complete Works in Verse and Prose of Samuel Daniel*, ed. Alexander S. Grosart (1885; New York: Russell and Russell, 1963).

Dekker, Thomas, *The Dramatic Works of Thomas Dekker*, ed. Fredson Bowers, 4 vols (Cambridge: Cambridge University Press, 1962).

Deloney, Thomas, *The Works of Thomas Deloney*, ed. Francis Oscar Mann (Oxford: Clarendon Press, 1912).

Donne, John, *The Songs and Sonets of John Donne*, ed. Theodore Redpath (1956; repr. London: Methuen, 1967).

Dryden, John, *The Prologues and Epilogues of John Dryden: A Critical

Edition, ed. William Bradford Gardner (New York: Columbia University Press, 1951).

Elizabeth I, *The Letters of Queen Elizabeth*, ed. G. B. Harrison (London: Cassell, 1935).

Elizabethan Critical Essays, ed. G. Gregory Smith, 2 vols (1904; repr. London: Oxford University Press, 1950).

Erasmus, Desiderius, *The Praise of Folly*, trs. and ed. Hoyt Hopewell Hudson (1941; repr. Princeton, N. J.: Princeton University Press, 1969).

Florio, John, *Queen Anna's New World of Words* . . . (1611; facsimile repr. London: Scolar Press, 1968).

Hawes, Stephen, *The Pastime of Pleasure*, ed. William Edward Mead, Early English Text Society, vol. CLXXIII (London: Oxford University Press, 1928).

Jocelin, Elizabeth, *The Mothers Legacie, To Her Unborne Childe* (London, 1624).

Lyly, John, *Euphues, the Anatomy of Wyt* (London, n.d. [1578]).

——, *Euphues and his England*, 2nd edn (London, 1606).

Marlowe, Christopher, *Hero and Leander* (London, 1598).

Middleton, Thomas, *The Ghost of Lucrece* (1600) ed. Joseph Quincy Adams (facsimile repr. New York: Charles Scribner's Sons, 1937).

Milton, John, *Poetical Works of John Milton*, ed. Helen Darbishire, 2 vols (Oxford: Clarendon Press, 1962).

——, *Milton's Prose*, ed. Malcolm W. Wallace (1925; repr. London: Oxford University Press, 1959).

Munda, Constantia, *The Worming of a Mad Dogge: or, a Soppe for Cerberus the Jaylor of Hell. No Confutation but a Sharpe Redargution of the Bayter of Women* (London, 1617).

Nashe, Thomas, *The Works of Thomas Nashe*, ed. Ronald B. McKerrow (Oxford: Basil Blackwell, 1958).

Pope, Alexander, *The Poems of Alexander Pope*, ed. John Butt (1963; repr. London: Methuen, 1965).

Popol Vuh: The Sacred Book of the Ancient Quiché Maya, trs. Sylvanus Morley and Delia Goetz (Norman: University of Oklahoma Press, 1956).

Raynalde, Thomas, *The Byrth of Mankynde, otherwyse named The Womans Booke*, 3rd edn (London, 1560).

Rich, Barnabe, *The Excellency of Good Women. The Honour and Estimation that Belongeth unto Them. The Infallible Markes Whereby to Know Them* (London, 1613).

Shakespeare, William, *The Complete Plays and Poems of William Shakespeare*, ed. William Allen Neilson and Charles Jarvis Hill (Cambridge, Mass.: Houghton Mifflin, 1942).

——, *King Lear*, New Arden edn, ed. Kenneth Muir (1964; repr. London: Methuen, 1969):

——, *Love's Labour's Lost*, New Arden edn, ed. Richard David (London: Methuen, 1968).

——, *Measure for Measure*, New Arden edn, ed. J. W. Lever (London: Methuen, 1967).

——, and Fletcher, John, *The Two Noble Kinsmen*, ed. G. L. Proudfoot (Lincoln, Nebr.: University of Nebraska Press, 1970).

Sidney, Sir Philip, *The Countess of Pembrokes Arcadia* (London, 1590).

——, *Astrophel and Stella* (London, 1591).

——, *The Defence of Poesie* (London, 1595).

Sowernam, Ester, *Ester Hath Hang'd Haman: or An Answere to a Lewd Pamphlet, entituled, The Arraignment of Women. With the Arraignment of Lewd, Idle, Froward, and Unconstant men, and Husbands . . .* (London, 1617).

Speght, Rachel, *A Mouzell for Melastomus. The Cynicall Bayter of, and Foule Mouthed Barker against Evahs Sex. Or an Apologeticall Answere to that Irreligious and Illiterate Pamphlet Made by Jo[seph]. Sw[etnam]. and by Him Intituled, The Arraignement of Women* (London, 1617).

Spenser, Edmund, *The Shepheardes Calender* (London, 1579).

——, *Fowre Hymnes* (London, 1596).

Swetnam, Joseph, *The Araignment of Lewde, Idle, Froward, and Unconstant Women: Or the Vanitie of Them, Choose You Whether. With a Commendacion of Wise, Vertuous and Honest Women. Pleasant for Married Men, Profitable for Young Men, and Hurtfull to None* (London, 1615).

Turberville, George, *Epitaphes, Epigrams, Songs and Sonets* (London, 1567).

Vicary, Thomas, *The Anatomie of the Bodie of Man*, 2nd edn, ed. Frederick J. Furnivall and Percy Furnivall (1577; repr. London: N. Trübner, 1888).

Whetstone, George, *The Rocke of Regard* (London, 1576).

Wilson, Thomas, *The Arte of Rhetorique* (London, 1553).

Zepheria (London, 1594).

SECONDARY WORKS

1. *REFERENCE*

An Anthology of Elizabethan Dedications and Prefaces, ed. Clara Gebert (Philadelphia: University of Pennsylvania Press, 1963).

Brown, Mary Elizabeth (comp.), *Dedications: An Anthology of the Forms Used from the Earliest Days of Book-Making to the Present Time* (1913; repr. New York: Burt Franklin, 1964). Bibliography and Reference Series, no. 55.

Dobson, E. J., *English Pronunciation 1500–1700*, 2 vols (Oxford: Clarendon Press, 1957).

Ellis, Herbert A., *Shakespeare's Lusty Punning in 'Love's Labour's Lost'* (The Hague and Paris: Mouton, 1973).

Funk and Wagnalls Standard Dictionary of Folklore, Mythology, and Legend, ed. Maria Leach, 2 vols (New York: Funk and Wagnalls, 1949).

Grierson, Sir Herbert J. C., and Wason, Sandy, *The First and Last Note: or, First and Last Words from Prefaces, Introductions, Dedications, Epilogues* (London: Chatto & Windus, 1946).

Harbage, Alfred, *Annals of English Drama 975–1700*, 2nd edn, revised by Samuel Schoenbaum (Philadelphia: University of Pennsylvania Press, 1964).

Hazlitt, W. Carew, *Faiths and Folklore of the British Isles: A Descriptive and Historical Dictionary* (1870; repr. New York: Benjamin Blom, 1905).

Jobes, Gertrude, *Dictionary of Mythology, Folklore, and Symbols*, 3 vols (New York: Scarecrow Press, 1962).

Knapp, Mary Ellen, *Prologues and Epilogues of the Eighteenth Century*, Yale Studies in English, vol. CXLIX (New Haven, Conn.: Yale University Press, 1961).

Kökeritz, Helge, *Shakespeare's Pronunciation*, 2nd edn (New Haven, Conn.: Yale University Press, 1960).

Larousse Encyclopaedia of Mythology (New York: Prometheus Press, 1960).

Partridge, Eric, *Shakespeare's Bawdy*, 2nd edn (New York: E. P. Dutton, 1969).

Robbins, Rossell Hope, *The Encyclopaedia of Witchcraft and Demonology* (London: Peter Nevill, 1969).

Schiller, Gertrud, *Iconography of Christian Art*, vol. I, trs. Janet

Seligman (1966; repr. Greenwich, Conn.: New York Graphic Society, 1971).

Schoenbaum, Samuel, *William Shakespeare: A Documentary Life* (New York: Oxford University Press in association with The Scolar Press, 1975).

The Shakespeare Allusion-Book: A Collection of Allusions to Shakespeare from 1591 to 1700, ed. John Munro (London: Chatto & Windus, 1909).

Skeat, W. W., *Etymological Dictionary of the English Language*, 4th edn (Oxford: Clarendon Press, 1974).

Thrall, William Flint *et al.*, *A Handbook to Literature* (New York: Odyssey Press, 1960).

Utley, Francis Lee, *The Crooked Rib: An Analytical Index to the Argument about Women in English and Scots Literature to the End of the Year 1598* (1944; repr. New York: Octagon Books, 1970).

Wheatley, Henry Benjamin, *The Dedication of Books to Patron and Friend: A Chapter in Literary History* (London: E. Stock, 1887).

Wickham, Glynne, *Early English Stages: 1300 to 1600*, 2 vols (New York: Columbia University Press, 1963).

Williams, Franklin Burleigh, *Index of Dedications and Commendatory Verses in English Books Before 1641* (London: Bibliographical Society, 1962).

2. *MEDICAL, SOCIOLOGICAL AND ANTHROPOLOGICAL STUDIES*

Anderson, Ruth Leila, *Elizabethan Psychology and Shakespeare's Plays* (1927; repr. New York: Haskell House, 1964).

Babb, Lawrence, *The Elizabethan Malady: A Study of Melancholia in English Literature from 1580 to 1642* (1951; repr. East Lansing: Michigan State University Press, 1965).

Briffault, Robert, *The Mothers*, ed. Gordon Rattray Taylor (1927; New York: Grosset and Dunlap, 1959).

Clarke, Edwin and Dewhurst, Kenneth, *An Illustrated History of Brain Function* (Oxford: Sanford Publications, 1972).

The History and Philosophy of Knowledge of the Brain and Its Functions (1958; repr. Amsterdam: B. M. Israel, 1973).

Legman, Gershon, *Rationale of the Dirty Joke: An Analysis of Sexual Humor* (New York: Grove Press, 1968).

O'Neill, Ynez Violé, 'William of Conches and the Cerebral Membranes', *Clio Medica*, II (1967) 13–21.

Overholster, Winifred, 'Shakespeare's Psychiatry – and After', *SQ*, x (1959) 335–52.
Oyle, Irving M D, *Time, Space and the Mind* (Millbrae, Calif.: Celestial Arts, 1976).
Roheim, Geza, *The Origin and Function of Culture* (1968; repr. New York: Anchor Books, 1971).
Schäfer, Jürgen, 'When They Marry, They Get Wenches', *SQ*, xxii (1971) 203–11.
Taylor, Gordon Rattray, *Sex in History* (1953; repr. London: Harper and Row, 1973).
Wright, Celeste Turner, 'The Amazons in Elizabethan Literature', *SP*, xxxvii (1940) 433–56.
——, 'Something More About Eve', *SP*, xli (1944) 156–68.
——, 'The Elizabethan Female Worthies', *SP*, xliii (1946) 629–43.

3. *SHAKESPEARIAN CRITICISM*

A. GENRES OR MISCELLANEOUS GROUPINGS OF PLAYS

Berry, Ralph, *Shakespeare's Comedies: Explorations in Form* (Princeton, N. J.: Princeton University Press, 1972).
Charney, Maurice, *Shakespeare's Roman Plays: The Function of Imagery in the Drama* (Cambridge, Mass.: Harvard University Press, 1961).
——, *Discussions of Shakespeare's Roman Plays* (Boston, Mass.: D. C. Heath, 1961).
Coghill, Neville, 'The Basis of Shakespearian Comedy: A Study in Mediaeval Affinities', in *Essays and Studies, 1950* (London: John Murray, 1950) vol. iii, pp. 1–28.
Hoyle, James, 'Some Emblems in Shakespeare's Henry IV Plays', *ELH*, xxxviii (1971) 512–27.
Hubbell, Lindley Williams, *A Note on the Shakespeare Apocrypha*, 2nd edn, augmented (Kobe, Japan: Ikuta Press, 1972).
Hunter, Robert Grams, *Shakespeare and the Comedy of Forgiveness* (New York: Columbia University Press, 1965).
James, D. G., *The Dream of Learning: An Essay on 'The Advancement of Learning', 'Hamlet' and 'King Lear'* (Oxford: Clarendon Press, 1951).
Kirsch, James, *Shakespeare's Royal Self* (New York: G. P. Putnam's Sons, for the C. G. Jung Foundation for Analytical Psychology, 1966).

Knight, G. Wilson, *The Crown of Life: Essays in Interpretation of Shakespeare's Final Plays* (1947; repr. New York: Barnes and Noble, 1966).

La Guardia, Eric, 'Ceremony and History: The Problem of Symbol from *Richard II* to *Henry V* ', in *Pacific Coast Studies in Shakespeare*, ed. Waldo McNeir and Thelma N. Greenfield (Eugene: University of Oregon Books, 1966) pp. 68–88.

Lascelles, Mary, *Shakespeare's Comic Insight*, Proceedings of the British Academy, vol. XLVIII (London: Oxford University Press, 1962).

Lawrence, William Witherle, *Shakespeare's Problem Comedies*, 2nd edn (New York: Frederick Ungar, 1960).

Levin, R. A., '*Twelfth Night, The Merchant of Venice*, and Two Alternative Approaches to Shakespearean Comedy', *ES*, LIX (1978) 336–43.

Muir, Kenneth, *Shakespeare and the Tragic Pattern*, Proceedings of the British Academy, vol. XLIV (London: Oxford University Press, 1958).

——, *Shakespeare as Collaborator* (London: Methuen, 1960).

Smith, Hallett, 'Shakespeare's Romances', *HLQ*, XXVII (1963–4) 279–87.

Tillyard, E. M. W., *Shakespeare's Problem Plays* (London: Chatto & Windus, 1950).

Traversi, Derek, *Shakespeare from 'Richard II' to 'Henry V'* (1957; repr. Stanford, Calif.: Stanford University Press, 1968).

——, *Shakespeare: The Last Phase* (1955; repr. Stanford, Calif.: Stanford University Press, 1969).

Velie, Alan R., *Shakespeare's Repentance Plays: The Search for an Adequate Form* (Teaneck, N. J.: Fairleigh Dickinson University Press, 1972).

Welsh, Alexander, 'The Loss of Men and Getting of Children: *All's Well That Ends Well* and *Measure for Measure*', *MLR*, LXXIII (1978) 17–28.

Willcock, Gladys D., *Language and Poetry in Shakespeare's Early Plays*, Proceedings of the British Academy, vol. XL (London: Geoffrey Cumberlege, 1954).

B. INDIVIDUAL PLAYS (ARRANGED ALPHABETICALLY)

All's Well That Ends Well
Adams, John F., '*All's Well That Ends Well*: The Paradox of

Procreation', *SQ*, XII (1961) 261–71.

Calderwood, James A., 'The Mingled Yarn of *All's Well*', *JEGP*, LXII (1963) 61–76.

Donaldson, James A., '*All's Well That Ends Well*: Shakespeare's Play of Endings', *EIC*, XXVII (1977) 34–55.

Halio, Jay L., '*All's Well That Ends Well*', *SQ*, XV (1964) 33–43.

Shapiro, 'Michael, '"The Web of our Life": Human Frailty and Mutual Redemption in *All's Well That Ends Well*', *JEGP*, LXXI (1972) 512–26.

As You Like It
Jenkins, Harold, '*As You Like It*', *ShS*, VIII (1955) 40–51.

Kuhn, Maura Slattery, 'Much Virtue in *If*', *SQ*, XXVIII (1977) 40–50.

Coriolanus
Barron, David B., '*Coriolanus*: Portrait of the Artist as Infant', *AI*, XIX (1962) 171–93.

Maxwell, James C., 'Animal Imagery in *Coriolanus*', *MLR*, XLII (1947) 417–21.

McCanles, Michael, 'The Dialectic of Transcendence in Shakespeare's *Coriolanus*', *PMLA*, LXXXII (1967) 44–53.

Cymbeline
Thorne, William B., '*Cymbeline*: "Lopp'd Branches" and the Concept of Regeneration', *SQ*, XX (1969) 143–59.

Hamlet
Altick, Richard D., '*Hamlet* and the Odor of Mortality', *SQ*, V (1954) 167–76.

Camden, Carroll, 'On Ophelia's Madness', *SQ*, XV (1964) 247–55.

Gibson, Evan K., '"Conception Is a Blessing"', *PMLA*, LXIV (1949) 1236–8.

Hammersmith, James P., '*Hamlet* and the Myth of Memory', *ELH*, XLV (1978) 597–607.

Hankins, John E., 'Hamlet's "God Kissing Carrion": A Theory of the Generation of Life', *PMLA*, LXIV (1949) 507–16.

Hunter, G. K., '*Hamlet* Criticism', *CritQ*, I (1959) 27–32.

Johnson, S. F., 'The Regeneration of Hamlet', *SQ*, III (1952) 187–207.

Maxwell, Baldwin, 'Hamlet's Mother', *SQ*, XV (1964) 235–46.

Morris, Harry, '*Hamlet* as a *Memento Mori* Poem', *PMLA*, LXXXV (1970) 1035–40.

Muir, Kenneth, 'Imagery and Symbolism in *Hamlet*', *EA*, XVII (1964) 353–63.

Phialas, Peter G., 'Hamlet and the Grave-Maker', *JEGP*, LXIII (1964) 226–34.

Westlund, Joseph R., 'Ambivalence in the Player's Speech in *Hamlet*', *SEL*, XVIII (1978) 246–56.

Henry V

Hobday, C. H., 'Imagery and Irony in *Henry V*', *ShS*, XXI (1968) 107–13.

Henry VI

Bevington, David M., 'The Domineering Female in *1 Henry VI*', *ShS*, II (1967) 51–8.

Calderwood, James L., 'Shakespeare's Evolving Imagery: *2 Henry VI*', *ES*, XLVIII (1967) 481–93.

Henry VIII

Cox, John D., '*Henry VIII* and the Masque', *ELH*, XLV (1978) 390–409.

Felperin, Howard, 'Shakespeare's *Henry VIII*: History as Myth', *SEL*, VI (1966) 225–46.

Mincoff, Marco, '*Henry VIII* and Fletcher', *SQ*, XII (1961) 239–61.

McBride, Tom, '*Henry VIII* as Machiavellian Romance', *JEGP*, LXXVI (1977) 26–39.

Richmond, H. M., 'Shakespeare's *Henry VIII*: Romance Redeemed by History', *ShakS*, IV (1968) 334–49.

Tillyard, E. M. W., 'Why Did Shakespeare Write *Henry VIII*?', *CritQ*, III (1961) 22–7.

King John

Stevick, Robert D., ' "Repentant Ashes": The Matrix of "Shakespearean" Poetic Language', *SQ*, XIII (1962) 366–70.

King Lear

Elton, William R., *King Lear and the Gods* (San Marino, Calif.: The Huntington Library, 1966).

Greenfield, Thelma Neilson, 'The Clothing Motif in *King Lear*', *SQ*, V (1954) 281–6.

Heilman, Robert Bechtold, *This Great Stage: Image and Structure in 'King Lear'* (1948; repr. Seattle: University of Washington Press, 1963).

Jorgensen, Paul A., *Lear's Self-Discovery* (Berkeley, Calif.: University of California Press, 1967).

Kanzer, Mark; 'Imagery in *King Lear*', *AI*, xxii (1965) 3–13.

Keast, W. R., 'Imagery and Meaning in the Interpretation of *Lear*', *MP*, xlvii (1949) 45–64.

Mack, Maynard, *'King Lear' in Our Time* (Berkeley, Calif.: University of California Press, 1965).

Rosenberg, Marvin, *The Masks of King Lear* (Berkeley, Calif.: University of California Press, 1972).

West, Robert H., 'Sex and Pessimism in *King Lear*', *SQ*, xi (1960) 55–60.

Love's Labour's Lost

Agnew, Gates K., 'Berowne and the Progress of *Love's Labour's Lost*', *ShakS*, iv (1969) 40–72.

Anderson, J. J., 'The Morality of *Love's Labour's Lost*', *ShS*, xxiv (1971) 55–62.

Berry, Ralph, 'The Words of Mercury', *ShS*, xxii (1969) 69–74.

Calderwood, James L., *'Love's Labour's Lost*: A Wantoning with Words', *SEL*, v (1965) 317–32.

Evans, Malcolm, 'Mercury versus Apollo: A Reading of *Love's Labour's Lost*', *SQ*, xxvi (1975) 113–27.

Hawkes, Terence, 'Shakespeare's Talking Animals', *ShS*, xxiv (1971) 47–54.

Lennam, Trevor, ' "The Ventricle of Memory": Wit and Wisdom in *Love's Labour's Lost*', *SQ*, xxiv (1973) 54–61.

McLay, Catherine M., 'The Dialogues of Spring and Winter: A Key to the Unity of *Love's Labour's Lost*', *SQ*, xviii (1967) 119–28.

Westlund, Joseph, 'Fancy and Achievement in *Love's Labour's Lost*', *SQ*, xviii (1967) 37–46.

Macbeth

Allen, Michael J. B., 'Macbeth's Genial Porter', *ELR*, iv (1974) 326–36.

Barron, David B., 'The Babe That Milks: An Organic Study of *Macbeth*', *AI*, xvii (1960) 133–61.

Biggins, Dennis, 'Sexuality, Witchcraft, and Violence in *Macbeth*', *ShakS*, viii (1975) 255–78.

Brooks, Cleanth, 'The Naked Babe and the Cloak of Manliness', in *The Well-Wrought Urn: Studies in the Structure of Poetry* (New York: Harcourt, Brace, 1947) pp. 21–46.

Dyson, J. P., 'The Structural Function of the Banquet Scene in *Macbeth*', *SQ*, xiv, (1963) 369–78.

Goode, Bill, 'How Little the Lady Knew Her Lord: A Note on *Macbeth*', *AI*, xx (1963) 349–86.

Harcourt, John B., 'I Pray You, Remember the Porter', *SQ*, xii (1961) 392–402.

Hyman, Lawrence W., '*Macbeth*: The Hand and the Eye', *TSL*, v (1960) 97–100.

Kocher, Paul H., 'Lady Macbeth and the Doctor', *SQ*, v (1954) 341–9.

Silling, Edward, 'Another Meaning for "Breech'd"', *MSE*, iv (1974) no. 3, 56.

Tromly, Frederic B., 'Macbeth and His Porter', *SQ*, xxii (1975) 151–6.

Measure for Measure

Altieri, Joanne, 'Style and Social Disorder in *Measure for Measure*', *SQ*, xxv (1974) 6–16.

Battenhouse, Roy W., '*Measure for Measure* and the Christian Doctrine of Atonement', *PMLA*, lxi (1946) 1029–59.

Black, James, 'The Unfolding of *Measure for Measure*', *ShS*, xxvi (1972) 119–28.

Coghill, Neville, 'Comic Form in *Measure for Measure*', *ShS*, xxviii (1974) 14–27.

Dunkel, Wilbur D., 'Law and Equity in *Measure for Measure*', *SQ*, xiii (1962) 275–85.

Grivelet, Michel, ' "And Measure Still for Measure": sur quelques études récentes de la pièce de Shakespeare', *EA*, xxi (1968) 65–72.

Hyman, Lawrence W., 'The Unity of *Measure for Measure*', *MLQ*, xxxvi (1975) 3–20.

Krieger, Murray, '*Measure for Measure* and Elizabethan Comedy', *PMLA*, lxvi (1951) 775–84.

Lawrence, William W., '*Measure for Measure* and Lucio', *SQ*, ix (1958) 443–53.

Leech, Clifford, 'The "Meaning" of *Measure for Measure*', *ShS*, iii (1950) 66–73.

Owen, Lucy, 'Mode and Character in *Measure for Measure*', *SQ*, xxv (1974) 17–32.

Partee, Morris Henry, 'The Comic Unity of *Measure for Measure*', *Genre*, VI (1973) 274–93.

Pope, E. M., 'The Renaissance Background of *Measure for Measure*', *ShS*, II (1949) 66–82.

Price, Jonathan R., '*Measure for Measure* and the Critics: Towards a New Approach', *SQ*, XX (1969) 178–204.

Sypher, Wylie, 'Shakespeare as Casuist: *Measure for Measure*', *SR*, LVIII (1950) 262–80.

Trombetta, James S., 'Versions of Dying in *Measure for Measure*', *ELR*, VI (1976) 60–76.

Weil, Herbert J., Jr, 'Form and Contexts in *Measure for Measure*', *CritQ*, XII (1970) 55–62.

The Merchant of Venice
Donow, Herbert S., 'Shakespeare's Caskets: Unity in *The Merchant of Venice*', *ShakS*, IV (1969) 86–98.

The Merry Wives of Windsor
Roberts, Jeanne Addison, '*The Merry Wives*: Suitably Shallow, but neither Simple nor Slender', *ShakS*, VI (1972) 109–23.

A Midsummer Night's Dream
Dent, R. W., 'Imagination in *A Midsummer Night's Dream*', *SQ*, XV (1964) 115–29.

Gui, Weston A., 'Bottom's Dream', *AI*, IX (1952) 246–305.

Vlasopoulos, Anca, 'The Ritual of Midsummer: A Pattern for *A Midsummer Night's Dream*', *RenQ*, XXXI (1978) no. 2, 21–9.

Much Ado About Nothing
Everett, Barbara, '*Much Ado About Nothing*', *CritQ*, III (1961) 319–34.

Lewalski, Barbara K., 'Hero's Name – and Namesake – in *Much Ado About Nothing*', *ELN*, VII (1970) no. 3, 175–9.

Wain, John, 'The Shakespearean Lie-Detector: Thoughts on *Much Ado About Nothing*', *CritQ*, IX (1967) 27–42.

Othello
Boose, Lynda E., 'Othello's Handkerchief: "The Recognizance and Pledge of Love"', *ELR*, V (1975) 360–74.

——, '"Lust in Action": *Othello* as Shakespeare's Tragedy of Human Sexuality' (unpublished dissertation, University of California at Los Angeles, 1976).

Camden, Carroll, 'Iago on Women', *JEGP*, XLVIII (1949) 57–71.

De Mendonça, Barbara Heliodora C., '*Othello*: A Tragedy Built on Comic Structure', *ShS*, XXI (1968) 31–8.

Everett, Barbara, 'Reflections on the Sentimentalist's *Othello*', *CritQ*, III (1961) 127–39.

Fraser, John, '*Othello* and Honour', *Critical Review*, VIII (1965) 59–70.

Garnier, S. N., 'Shakespeare's Desdemona', *ShakS*, IX (1976) 233–52.

Heilman, Robert B., *Magic in the Web* (Lexington: University of Kentucky Press, 1956).

Jorgensen, Paul A., ' "Perplex'd in the Extreme": The Role of Thought in *Othello*', *SQ*, XV (1964) 265–75.

Mercer, Peter, '*Othello* and the Form of Heroic Tragedy', *CritQ*, XI (1969) 45–61.

Money, John, 'Othello's "It is the Cause . . . ." An Analysis', *ShS*, VI (1953) 94–105.

Rogers, Robert H., 'Endopsychic Drama in *Othello*', *SQ*, XX (1969) 205–15.

Rosenberg, Marvin, 'In Defense of Iago', *SQ*, VI (1955) 145–58.

Snyder, Susan, '*Othello* and the Conventions of Romantic Comedy', *RenD*, V (1972) 123–41.

Wall, John N., 'Shakespeare's Aural Art: The Metaphor of the Ear in *Othello*', *SQ*, XXX (1979) no. 3, 358–66.

Pericles

Felperin, Howard, 'Shakespeare's Miracle Play', *SQ*, XVIII (1967) 363–74.

Flower, Annette C., 'Disguise and Identity in *Pericles, Prince of Tyre*', *SQ*, XXV (1975) 39–41.

Thorne, W. B., '*Pericles* and the Incest-Fertility Opposition', *SQ*, XXII (1971) 43–56.

Wood, James O., 'The Running Image in *Pericles*', *ShakS;* V (1969) 240–52.

Richard II

Altick, Richard D., 'Symphonic Imagery in *Richard II*', *PMLA*, LXII (1947) 339–65.

Barkan, Leonard, 'The Theatrical Consistency of *Richard II*', *SQ*, XXIX (1978) no. 1, 5–19.

Grivelet, Michel, 'Shakespeare's "War With Time": The *Sonnets* and *Richard II*', *ShS*, XXIII (1970) 69–78.

Harris, Kathryn Montgomery, 'Sun and Water Imagery in *Richard II*: Its Dramatic Function', *SQ*, xxi (1970) 157–65.
Heninger, S. K., Jr, 'The Sun-King Analogy in *Richard II*', *SQ*, xi (1960) 318–27.
Thompson, Karl F., 'Richard II, Martyr', *SQ*, viii (1957) 157–66.

Romeo and Juliet
Black, James, 'The Visual Artistry of *Romeo and Juliet*', *SEL*, xv (1975) 245–56.
Everett, Barbara, '*Romeo and Juliet*: The Nurse's Story', *CritQ*, xiv (1972) 129–39.
McArthur, Herbert, 'Romeo's Loquacious Friend', *SQ*, x (1959) 35–44.
Stewart, Stanley, 'Romeo and Necessity' in *Pacific Coast Studies in Shakespeare*, ed. Waldo F. McNeir and Thelma N. Greenfield (Eugene: University of Oregon Books, 1966) pp. 47–67.
Snyder, Susan, '*Romeo and Juliet*, Comedy into Tragedy', *EIC*, xx (1970) 391–401.
Thomas, Sydney, 'The Queen Mab Speech in *Romeo and Juliet*', *ShS*, xxv (1972) 73–80.

The Taming of the Shrew
Huston, Dennis J., ' "To Make a Puppet": Play and Play-Making in *The Taming of the Shrew*', *ShakS*, ix (1976) 73–85.
Heilman, Robert B., 'The Taming Untamed, or, The Return of the Shrew', *MLQ*, xxvii (1966) 147–61.

The Tempest
Davidson, Frank, '*The Tempest*: An Interpretation', *JEGP*, lxii (1963) 501–17.
Fitz, Linda Taylor, 'The Vocabulary of The Tempest' (Dissertation, University of California at Los Angeles, 1970).

Timon of Athens
Draper, R. P., '*Timon of Athens*', *SQ*, viii (1957) 195–200.
Merchant, W. M., '*Timon* and the Conceit of Art', *SQ*, vi (1955) 249–57.

Titus Andronicus
Waith, Eugene M., 'The Metamorphosis of Violence in *Titus Andronicus*', *ShS*, x (1957) 39–49.

Willbern, David, 'Rape and Revenge in *Titus Andronicus*', *ELR*, VIII (1978) no. 2, 159–82.

Troilus and Cressida
McAlindon, T., 'Language, Style and Meaning in *Troilus and Cressida*', *PMLA*, LXXXIV (1969) 29–43.

Twelfth Night
Adams, Barry B., 'Orsino and the Spirit of Love', *SQ*, XXIX (1978) no. 1, 52–9.
Huston, Dennis J., 'When I Came To Man's Estate: *Twelfth Night* and Problems of Identity', *MLQ*, XXXIII (1972) 274–88.
Kelly, T. F., '*Twelfth Night*', *Critical Review*, XIX (1977) 54–70.
Palmer, D. J., 'Art and Nature in *Twelfth Night*', *CritQ*, IX (1970) 201–12.

The Two Gentlemen of Verona
Danby, John F., 'Shakespeare Criticism and *Two Gentlemen of Verona*', *CritQ*, II (1950) 309–21.

The Two Noble Kinsmen
Bertram, Paul, *Shakespeare and The Two Noble Kinsmen* (New Brunswick, N. J.: Rutgers University Press, 1965).
Mincoff, Marco, 'The Authorship of *The Two Noble Kinsmen*', *ES*, XXXIII (1952) 97–115.

The Winter's Tale
Gourlay, Patricia Southard, ' "O my most sacred Lady": Female Metaphor in *The Winter's Tale*', *ELR*, V (1975) 375–95.
Hartwig, Joan, 'The Tragicomic Perspective of *The Winter's Tale*', *ELH*, XXXVII (1970) 12–36.
Hoeniger, David F., 'The Meaning of *The Winter's Tale*', *UTQ*, XX (1950) 11–26.
Lindenbaum, Peter, 'Time, Sexual Love, and the Uses of Pastoral in *The Winter's Tale*', *MLQ*, XXXIII (1972) 3–22.
Livingston, Mary L., 'The Natural Art of *The Winter's Tale*', *MLQ*, XXX (1969) 340–55.
Scott, William O., 'Seasons and Flowers in *The Winter's Tale*', *SQ*, XIV (1963) 411–17.
Siemon, James Edward, ' "But It Appears She Lives": Iteration in *The Winter's Tale*', *PMLA*, LXXXIX (1974) 10–16.

C. SHAKESPEARE'S LANGUAGE AND VERBAL
IMAGERY

(i) *General Studies*

Barton, Anne, 'Shakespeare and the Limits of Language', *ShS*, xxiv (1971) 20–30.

Clemen, Wolfgang H., *The Development of Shakespeare's Imagery* (1951; repr. London: Methuen, 1969).

Doran, Madeleine, *Shakespeare's Dramatic Language* (Madison: University of Wisconsin Press, 1976).

Hulme, Hilda M., *Explorations in Shakespeare's Language: Some Problems of Lexical Meaning in the Dramatic Text* (Aberdeen: Longman Green, 1962).

——, *Yours That Read Him: An Introduction to Shakespeare's Language* (London: Ginn, 1972).

Jorgensen, Paul A., *Redeeming Shakespeare's Words* (Berkeley, Calif.: University of California Press, 1962).

Joseph, Sister Miriam, *Shakespeare's Use of the Arts of Language* (New York: Harcourt, Brace and World, 1962).

Mahood, M. M., *Shakespeare's Wordplay* (London: Methuen, 1957).

Prior, Moody E., 'Imagery as a Test of Authorship', *SQ*, vi (1955) 381–6.

Spurgeon, Caroline F. E., *Shakespeare's Iterative Imagery*, Proceedings of the British Academy, vol. xvii (London: Oxford University Press, 1931).

——, *Shakespeare's Imagery and What It Tells Us* (1935; repr. Cambridge: Cambridge University Press, 1968).

Wentersdorf, Karl, 'Imagery as a Criterion of Authenticity: A Reconsideration of the Problem', *SQ*, xxiii (1972) 231–9.

Willcock, Gladys D., *Shakespeare as Critic of Language* (London: Oxford University Press, 1934).

(ii) *Specialised Studies*

Colman, E. A. M., *The Dramatic Uses of Bawdy in Shakespeare* (London: Longman, 1974).

Farrell, Kirby, *Shakespeare's Creation: The Language of Magic and Play* (Amherst: University of Massachusetts Press, 1975).

Gruttner, Tilo, *Buch und Schrift bei Shakespeare . . .* (Dissertation, Cologne, 1970; Chemnitz: n.d., n.p.).

Hankins, John Erskine, *Shakespeare's Derived Imagery* (Lawrence: University of Kansas Press, 1953).

Hudson, Kenneth, 'Shakespeare's Use of Colloquial Language', *ShS*, xxiii (1970) 39–48.
Vickers, Brian, *The Artistry of Shakespeare's Prose* (London: Methuen, 1968).

D. SHAKESPEARE'S DRAMATURGY AND VISUAL IMAGERY

Doebler, John, *Shakespeare's Speaking Pictures: Studies in Iconic Imagery* (Albuquerque: University of New Mexico Press, 1974).
Ewbank, Inga-Stina, ' "More Pregnantly Than Words": Some Uses and Limitations of Visual Symbolism', *ShS*, xxiv (1971) 13–18.
Pellegrini, G., 'Symbols and Significances', *ShS*, xvii (1964) 180–7.
Stoll, Elmer Edgar, 'Symbolism in Shakespeare', *MLR*, xlii (1947) 9–23.

E. SHAKESPERIAN THEMES AND SPECIAL TOPICS

Armstrong, E. A., *Shakespeare's Imagination* (London: Lindsay Drummond, 1946).
Clemen, Wolfgang H., *Shakespeare's Soliloquies* (Cambridge: Cambridge University Press, 1964).
Doran, Madeleine, 'The Idea of Excellence in Shakespeare', *SQ*, xxvii (1976) 133–49.
Dusinberre, Juliet, *Shakespeare and the Nature of Women* (London: Macmillan, 1975).
Edgar, Irving I., *Shakespeare, Medicine and Psychiatry: An Historical Study in Criticism and Interpretation* (New York: Philosophical Library, 1970).
Garber, Marjorie B., *Dream in Shakespeare: From Metaphor to Metamorphosis* (New Haven, Conn.: Yale University Press, 1974).
Grebanier, Bernard, *Then Came Each Actor: Shakespearean Actors, Great and Otherwise . . .* (New York: David McKay, 1975).
Harding, D. W., 'Women's Fantasy of Manhood: A Shakespearian Theme', *SQ*, xx (1969) 245–53.
McMichael, George, and Edgar M. Glenn (eds), *Shakespeare and His Rivals: A Casebook on the Authorship Controversy* (New York: Odyssey Press, 1962).
Mandel, Jerome, 'Dream and Imagination in Shakespeare', *SQ*, xxiv (1973) 61–8.
Ridley, M. R., *On Reading Shakespeare*, Proceedings of the British

Academy, vol. XXXVI (London: Humphrey Milford, 1940).

Rylands, George, *Shakespeare's Poetic Energy*, Proceedings of the British Academy, vol. XXXVII (London: Geoffrey Cumberlege, 1970).

Soellner, Rolf, *Shakespeare's Patterns of Self-Knowledge* (Columbus: Ohio State University Press, 1972).

Spencer, Theodore, *Shakespeare and the Nature of Man* (New York: Macmillan, 1942).

Sweet, George Elliott, *Shake-speare: The Mystery* (Stanford, Calif.: Stanford University Press, 1956).

Toliver, Harold, 'Shakespeare and the Abyss of Time', *JEGP*, LXIV (1965) 234–53.

Wain, John, 'The Mind of Shakespeare', in *More Talking of Shakespeare*, ed. John Garrett (1959; repr. Freeport: Books for Libraries Press, 1970).

Yoder, Audrey, *Animal Analogy in Shakespeare's Character Portrayal* (Columbia: King's Crown Press, 1947).

4. *GENERAL, CULTURAL, AND THEATRICAL STUDIES*

Bolle, Kees M., 'Structures of Renaissance Mysticism', in *The Darker Vision of the Renaissance: Beyond the Fields of Reason*, ed. Robert S. Kinsman (Berkeley, Calif.: University of California Press, 1974) 119–45.

Bundy, Maurice W., ' "Invention" and "Imagination" in the Renaissance', *JEGP*, XXIX (1930) 535–45.

Condren, Edward I., 'The Troubadour and His Labor of Love', *Mediaeval Studies*, XXXIV (1972) 174–95.

Cook, Fredric, *Acting: Being Natural. Professional Artist Letter* (los Angeles: Los Angeles Academy of Dramatic Art) 17 Feb 1977.

Cruttwell, Patrick, *The Shakespearean Moment and Its Place in the Poetry of the 17th Century* (New York: Random House, 1960).

Cunningham, J. V., *Tradition and Poetic Structure* (Denver, Col.: Alan Swallow, 1960).

Fluchère, Henri, *Shakespeare and the Elizabethans*, trs. Guy Hamilton (New York: Hill and Wang, 1956).

Foss, Martin, *Symbol and Metaphor in Human Experience* (1949; repr. Lincoln, Nebr.: University of Nebraska Press, n.d.).

Greene, David, 'Exploring Music – Something of a Mystery', *Musical Heritage Review*, II, no. 16 (18 Dec 1978) p. 47.

Hunter, William B., 'Eve's Demonic Dream', *ELH*, xiii (1946) 255–65.

Jones, Richard Foster, *The Triumph of the English Language: A Survey of Opinions Concerning the Vernacular from the Introduction of Printing to the Restoration* (Stanford, Calif.: Stanford University Press, 1952).

Kelly, Henry Ansgar, *The Matrimonial Trials of Henry VIII* (Stanford, Calif.: Stanford University Press, 1976).

McCanles, Michael, 'The Literal and the Metaphorical: Dialectic or Interchange', *PMLA*, xci (1976) 279–90.

Rosky, William, 'Imagery in the English Renaissance', *SRen*, v (1958) 49–73.

Sypher, Wylie, *Four Stages of Renaissance Style: Transformations in Art and Literature 1400–1700* (New York: Doubleday, 1955).

Woodward, Kenneth, and Mark, Rachel L., 'What Mary Means Now', *Newsweek* (1), 1 Jan 1979 pp. 52–3.

Index